"Our Young Soldier"

Lieutenant Francis Simcoe, 6 June 1791–6 April 1812

"Our Young Soldier"

Lieutenant Francis Simcoe,
6 June 1791–6 April 1812

Mary Beacock Fryer

Dundurn Press
Toronto • Oxford

Designer: Ron & Ron Design and Photography
Printer: Webcom

Canadian Cataloguing in Publication Data

Fryer, Mary Beacock, 1929-
       "Our young soldier" : Lieutenant Francis Simcoe, 6 June 1791-6 April 1812

Includes bibliographical references and index.
ISBN 1-55002-270-9

I. Simcoe, Francis Gwillim, 1791-1812. 2. Soldiers–Canada–Biography.
3. Canada–History–1791-1841–Biography. 4. Great Britain–History–1789-1820–Biography.
I. Title

FC3071.1.S545F79 1996   971.03'2'092   C96-990063-5   F1058.S545F79

Publication was assisted by the **Canada Council**, the **Book Publishing Industry Development Program** of the **Department of Canadian Heritage**, and the **Ontario Arts Council**.

Care has been taken to trace the ownership of copyright material used in this book. The author and the publisher welcome any information enabling them to rectify any references or credit in subsequent editions.

Printed and bound in Canada

Dundurn Press	Dundurn Press	Dundurn Press
2181 Queen Street East	73 Lime Walk	250 Sonwil Drive
Suite 301	Headington, Oxford	Buffalo, NY
Toronto, Ontario, Canada	England	U.S.A. 14225
M4E 1E5	OX3 7AD	

Table of Contents

"I have an obligation to assist our young soldier."

Francis Lord Rawdon, 2nd Earl of Moira

Acknowledgements

Any biography of Francis Simcoe owes much to the writings of his mother, Elizabeth, to her dearest friend, Mary Anne Burges, and to many people in Great Britain and Canada. Hilary Arnold, of York, and Christopher Dracott, of Devonshire, were most generous at sharing their own research. Major George Stephens and Margaret J Mulligan sent valuable material and the cover illustration from the Royal Inniskilling Fusiliers Regimental Museum in Enniskillen, Northern Ireland. Leon Warmski, Jim Suderman and Katrin Cooper were invaluable in helping me with illustrations and with locating Francis Simcoe's letters, journals and maps at the Ontario Archives. Maria Nogueira, of the Portuguese Trade and Tourism Commission, Maria José Ibaney, of the Tourist Office of Spain, and Irma Ditchburn, Ontario Government Art Collection, lent photographs. The staff at Dundurn Press and the Metropolitan Toronto Library were wonderful as usual. Carl Benn, Curator of Fort York, read the manuscript and straightened out matters military. Anne Melvin, librarian, Royal Canadian Military Institute. My daughter Elswyth and son Alexander lent their expertise on the computer. My husband, Geoffrey, laboured over the maps with meticulous care. Last, of course, is Francis Simcoe himself, for his own writing and artwork.

Introduction

A map of Southern Ontario seems peppered with two names – and with many other people and places associated with them. One is John Graves Simcoe, the first lieutenant governor, his family and friends. The other is Arthur Wellesley Duke of Wellington, his family and many of his officers. Francis Gwillim Simcoe, our hero, was sired by the first, and commanded by the second.

Legion are the places named by, or in honour of, the Simcoe connection. Of the governor himself, we have Lake Simcoe (he insisted it was named after his father), Simcoe County and the town of Simcoe in Haldimand-Norfolk. His wife is remembered in the townships of East and West Gwillimbury, and Whitchurch, after the Gwillim home in Herefordshire. The United Counties of Leeds and Grenville are especially lucky with – Bastard, Burgess, Kitley, Wolford, Yonge, Escott.

Names associated with Wellington are also legion. Many places were renamed after the hero of the Peninsular War, and Waterloo (in the latter instance a county, a city and a township). In the former Wellington District (now mostly in Wellington County), we find the townships of Arthur, Wellesley, Mornington (the Iron Duke's father was Lord Mornington), Waterloo and Corunna. In addition to Wellington County, we find Wellington village in Prince Edward County, Wellington Square (now Burlington) and Kars. The last seems misplaced, but good folk along the Rideau River wanted Wellington. When they discovered the name had already been taken, they settled for the place where the Turks won a victory over the Russians in 1855. Pakenham township and village, in Lanark County are a reminder of Kitty, Wellington's Duchess.

Douro Township was named for the Portuguese river that flows into the sea at Porto (Oporto), and for Arthur Viscount Douro, Wellington's elder son. Picton recalls Sir Thomas, commander of the 3rd Division under Wellington. Kemptville honours Sir James Kempt, one of Picton's brigade commanders and governor in chief of Upper and Lower Canada in 1828. Sir John Colborne, another Peninsular War veteran, was lieutenant governor of Upper Canada (Ontario) 1828 to 1836 and commander of forces in both Canadas during the rebellions of 1837-1838. A township in Huron County, Colborne village in Northumberland County, and Port Colborne, a city on Lake Erie, commemorate Sir John.

Francis Rawdon Hastings, 2nd Earl of Moira, was Simcoe's brother in arms during the American Revolution, and Francis Simcoe's honorary regimental colonel. In Hastings County the Moira River has its headwaters in Rawdon Township and flows into the Bay of Quinte at Belleville

The Duke of Richmond, who was host to Francis Simcoe in Ireland in 1808, and at whose ball Wellington was taken by surprise by Napoleon in 1815, was governor in chief of the Canadas in 1818. Richmond is a township in Lennox and Addington County. Richmond village is southwest of Ottawa, while Richmond Hill is a city in the Regional Municipality of York. Charles Lennox, 4th Duke of Richmond came to a sad end. He was bitten by a pet fox that was rabid, and he died of hydrophobia, a year after he arrived in the Canadas.

The game could go on indefinitely. Moore Township in Lambton County was named for Sir John Moore. A second Corunna in Ontario, a village in Moore Township, lies beside the St. Clair River to the south of Sarnia.

Alas, little recalls Francis Simcoe. The governor named an island after him, but the location is obscure. Castle Frank, the Simcoes' summer home above the Don Valley, burned down in 1829. The name was kept alive by a street name, and by Toronto Transit Commission which called one of its subway stations Castle Frank, rather prosaic. We have Frankford, in Hastings County, apparently named by Sir Francis Bond Head, after himself. Frankville, in Kitley Township, Leeds and Grenville, is a more promising location, but the connection would be difficult to establish. Perhaps, someone who enjoys this deliberately popular biography will be tempted to use Francis Simcoe's name somewhere.

Major General John Graves Simcoe in a red coat. He wore green only for duty with the Queen's Rangers.

Part One
The Canada Years

Chapter 1
Of a Family, Letters and Journals

One could say that Francis Simcoe was born with a silver spoon in his mouth. Certainly for the first few years of his life he was a princeling, much in the public eye. He was also a child of remarkable and distinguished parents. His father, John Graves Simcoe, is best remembered as the first lieutenant governor of Ontario, then Upper Canada. His mother, Elizabeth Posthuma Gwillim, left her mark on the province through her many watercolour sketches, and the diary she kept during her five years of residence in the Canadas.

As governor, John Graves Simcoe was a forward-looking administrator, a man of vision. Yet he was first and foremost a soldier, a bold innovator and the daring leader of his Queen's Rangers, who rose to become a lieutenant general in the British army. His father was Captain John Simcoe, Royal Navy, who died aboard his ship *Pembroke*, off Anticosti Island in May 1759 while serving with General James Wolfe's expedition to capture Quebec. His mother was Katherine Stamford of Bath, a city already renowned for its architecture and healing waters. The captain and his lady were married in Bath Abbey in 1747. The future Governor Simcoe was the third of four sons; the first two died in infancy. John Graves was born at Cotterstock, Northamptonshire, in 1752, and his youngest brother, Percy, in 1754. After the death of their father, their mother moved to Exeter, territory more familiar to her, but she may have had an even more compelling motive. Near Hembury Fort, an ancient hill ruin outside Honiton, stood Hembury Fort House, within easy reach of Exeter. Here dwelt Admiral Samuel Graves, John Graves Simcoe's godfather. Samuel Graves and John Simcoe had been naval captains together and valued friends. Katherine Simcoe may have wanted to reside close enough to the admiral to ensure that he would take a lively interest in her sons. When John Graves was twelve, ten-year-old Percy drowned in the River Exe. The good will of Admiral Graves on behalf of her only surviving son was more important than ever to Mrs. Katherine Simcoe. Over the years a bond developed between godfather and godson.

At Hembury Fort House, John Graves Simcoe was destined to become acquainted with his future wife. Elizabeth Posthuma Gwillim, ten years his junior, was an only child, and the niece of the admiral through his marriage to her aunt, Margaret Spinckes. Elizabeth came from a military family. Her father was Thomas Gwillim, of the manor of Old Court, Whitchurch, Herefordshire, very close to the border of Wales, a logical place to find people with a Welsh surname. Thomas died in Germany early in 1762 while serving as the Lieutenant Colonel of the 50th Regiment of Foot. Prior to transferring to the 50th, Thomas had been the major of the 7th Royal Fusiliers, and had served under Wolfe at Quebec in 1759.

Her mother was Elizabeth Spinckes, of the manor of All Saints, Aldwinkle [Aldwincle], Northamptonshire. Elizabeth was born at Aldwinkle about 20 September 1762 and baptised on the 22nd. Her mother was laid in her grave on the 23rd.[1] Because the infant had been orphaned at birth, Elizabeth was given the middle name Posthuma. She was the sole heir to two well-to-do families, the Gwillims of Whitchurch, and the Spinckeses of Aldwinkle. She spent the first fourteen years of her life with her grandmother Jemima Spinckes, at Aldwinkle, paying many visits to Whitchurch. In1769, her mother's sister, Margaret, married Admiral Graves. Afterwards she paid visits to Hembury Fort House. Following the death of Grandmother Spinckes in 1776, Hembury Fort House became Elizabeth's main home.

Another major character in the story of Francis Simcoe was his mother's lifelong friend, Miss Mary Anne Burges, who resided in Devonshire, first at Tracey, and later at Ashfield. Both houses were within walking distance of Wolford Lodge, the Simcoe family home. Like Elizabeth, Mary Anne kept a diary during the five years of her friend's absence in the Canadas. From her letters, sent in packets to their mother, we learn how the four eldest children fared. They had been left behind because educating them would be very complicated in the Upper Canadian wilderness. Ranging in age from seven to three, they remained in the care of Mrs. Ann Hunt. She came highly recommended, the widow of a naval officer who had long ago served under Admiral Graves. The Simcoes hired her daughter Mary to be a tutor to the girls. She also became a sympathetic companion to them, and a close friend of Mary Anne Burges.

The two youngest Simcoe children, Sophia, almost two, and Francis, five months, went with their parents to Upper Canada. From Mary Anne's letters we learn something of Sophia, of Francis, and of the baby sister, Katherine, who was born and died during the Canada years. Their mother wrote little about the children in her original diary. In her letters Mary Anne was responding to letters which Elizabeth sent directly to her, which do not appear to have survived the centuries.

Mary Anne asked Elizabeth, "tell me all about Francis." Elizabeth apparently wrote nothing specific about the children lucky enough to be with her in the installments of the diary that she sent to Wolford Lodge. Her reticence could be explained by her awareness of how much the children left behind were missing her. She never mentioned her seventh child, Katherine, and only once did she refer to Sophia by name. Yet in the published version of her diary, we find many references to Francis. This has created a false impression that he was her favourite child. What seems to have occurred was that the information on Francis was lifted from Elizabeth's letters and incorporated into the diary by his sisters, after the family had lost the treasured eldest son. Mary Anne's

National Archives C81931

Elizabeth Simcoe by her friend Mary Anne Burges. Mistakenly, John Ross Robertson thought she was in Welsh dress. She is wearing a high fashion beaver hat over a lace mob cap.

letters show her reaction to Elizabeth's comments on Sophia's temper, but since Sophia was a party to alterations in the diary, negative sentiments were left where they were, probably at her request.

At first, Elizabeth speaks for Francis in her letters to Mary Anne, or to Mrs. Hunt. More of his life is revealed in the many letters the family wrote after their return to Devon.[2] Here is to be found a bright, lovable lad, who, despite an exotic past in Upper Canada, quickly made friends and adapted to new situations. His great aunt, Margaret Graves, wrote that his "liking Eaton [Eton] does him credit". By the time he is sixteen, a surprisingly literate Francis is sending letters regularly to his mother and sisters, and keeping a journal of his travels and daily life that is quite similar to his mother's Canadian diary,

For an unknown number of years these letters and journals reposed uncatalogued in the Ontario Archives. Since they did not relate specifically to Ontario topics, they may have been considered as of scant interest. They had been microfilmed along with the other Simcoe papers, but not organized. They were catalogued by 1988, and are now easier to find in the microfilm collection.[3]

From the various records, a mother's diary,[4] family letters from Devon, and papers in the Devon Record Office in Exeter, and Ontario Archives in Toronto, and genealogies of the Simcoe, Gwillim, Burges and Head families, emerges the saga of the infant in arms who travelled to Canada, who grew into a lively boy, and who showed the same kind of promise as his father. His was a life that led to Ireland, to the Spanish/Portuguese Peninsula, to Lord Wellington's table, and to Badajoz.

Chapter 2
The Simcoes of Wolford Lodge

The story of Francis Simcoe and of his immediate family really begins in the autumn of 1781 towards the end of the American Revolution. Following the British defeat at Yorktown, Virginia, Lieutenant Colonel John Graves Simcoe was invalided home in poor health. Wounded three times since he had arrived in the colonies in 1775 with the rank of captain, he had never made a full recovery. At the invitation of Admiral Graves and his wife, Elizabeth's Gwillim's Aunt Margaret, he came to Hembury Fort House to convalesce. Before long all parties agreed that the dashing commander of the Queen's Rangers, and Miss Gwillim, would make a suitable match. He was a promising soldier, with the prospect of an even more brilliant career ahead of him. She was a wealthy orphan who needed an honest husband, one who could be relied upon to look after her best interests. He was madly in love and demonstratively affectionate. On her part she respected him and was happy to become his helpmate. Although she was energetic, she maintained a cool detachment that seemed in stark contrast to her future husband's bubbling vitality.

As a child Elizabeth had had few playmates of like age. She spent most of her time in company with her governess, among adoring adults at her various homes. In consequence she was often perplexed by her children. The colonel, who as a child had been called "Graves" (John was reserved for his father), had known the rough and tumble of the Exeter Grammar School and Eton College. Close association with his contemporaries made him comfortable with most children and more playful than Elizabeth with his own.

The Simcoes were married, by licence, on 30 December 1782 in the Church of St. Mary and St. Giles, at Buckerell, Devon, the Graves' parish. Having a licence was the fashionable way. Reading of the banns was considered common, suitable only for the lower orders. The witnesses were Simcoe's godfather and Elizabeth's aunt. The groom would turn forty in February; the bride had celebrated her twentieth birthday the previous September. Both were dark eyed; his hair was brown, hers black. One of his officers in the Queen's Rangers described his colonel as tending to stoutness, and standing about five feet seven or eight inches, an average height for the time. Elizabeth was tiny and slim, with pointed facial features that gave her a lively appearance. She felt comfortable among women who were petite, like herself, and somewhat ill at ease with statuesque matrons who could gaze down at her. Her closest friend, Mary Anne Burges, was also short, but more inclined towards plumpness than Elizabeth.

According to the law of the day, when Elizabeth married she lost the right to control her own fortune. That right now belonged to her husband, Colonel Simcoe. (She referred to every adult by title, in the fashion of the characters drawn by her contemporary, Jane Austen. Thus Simcoe was Coll., or the Gov., and later the Genl., never "John" or "Graves".)

Simcoe was a man of principle. He saw in his duty as custodian of his wife's assets an obligation to ensure that they grew and were not dissipated on material things he might covet for himself. The first need was for a suitable home, one that would reflect their standing in the county. He purchased the manor known as Wolford Church, 5,000 beautiful acres on the River Wolf in the parish of Dunkeswell. The manor house, a single-storey sprawling structure in bad condition, stood three miles outside the lace-making town of Honiton. A first priority was the demolition of the old home, and the building of a stone country house with forty rooms on two stories. To begin with, he and Elizabeth took up residence in a rented house in Honiton. Because he knew little about agriculture and the running of a large estate, Simcoe hired John Scadding (1754 - 1824), who came highly recommended, as his manager. The Scaddings were well known to the residents of the Wolford manor. Thomas Scadding, John's brother, was one of the Simcoes' tenant farmers.

While making decisions about the estate and the building of the new house, Simcoe was also in frequent contact with Horse Guards, the headquarters of the War Office in London. He wanted to have his Queen's Rangers elevated to the British regular establishment. When he left on convalescent leave, the corps was ranked as a provincial one, and the officers were not entitled to the same benefits as those serving in numbered regiments that were included in The Army List. He was successful. As of 30 December 1782, five days after his marriage, the Rangers were considered British regulars, although the regiment was never numbered. On The Army List they are shown as "Simcoe's Rangers".[1]

Simcoe also busied himself with religion and politics. Possibly as a way of curbing the spread of Methodism, so popular in the West Country, both he and Elizabeth became evangelical Anglicans. They hoped to revitalize the established church through the teaching of the four gospels, through Biblical preaching, through a better educated clergy, and through missionary work by laymen like themselves that would persuade everyone in the parish to attend church regularly and live good lives.

The day began and ended with prayers. Attendance by all members of the family and servants was compulsory. To stress that this was a formal and important ceremony, all the servants on the estate had to form a line and march like soldiers into the drawing room where the family gathered first. Only the infirm were permitted to sit; all others remained standing except during prayers. When he was at home Colonel Simcoe himself read the lesson and led the prayers and the reciting of a psalm; in his absence Elizabeth performed the task. Evangelical work began in the home. Family members and servants were expected to reinforce their twice daily devotions by learning "off by heart" selected passages from the Old and New Testaments and the Book of Common Prayer. Both Simcoes believed in the sanctity of the Church of England, and therefore the sovereign as head of the church.

Like his sisters, Francis was instructed daily in these divine precepts. In time, his father hoped to build a chapel on the estate. The drawing room seemed too secular, too frivolous, for so sacred a duty as paying homage to the Creator and His Son.

Along with missionary work, Simcoe felt obliged to serve the public good, and a vital aspect was the future health of the British Empire. By 1790, he had a vision of Canada north of the Great Lakes not only as a haven for American Loyalists, but as the place to create a new Empire in North America, to make up for the one Britain had lost. To further this and other ambitions he stood for election in the riding of St. Mawes, Cornwall, and won the seat. The life of a country squire was agreeable, but Simcoe wanted a public appointment. The best route was through membership in Parliament. Another involved cultivating influential friends. Two such were Mary Anne's brother, Sir James Bland Burges, Under Secretary for Foreign Affairs, and Henry Addington, a future prime minister.

Meanwhile, the new home, Wolford Lodge, had been completed and the family had been in residence in the stone mansion for some six years. The colonel and his wife were by then the proud parents of five daughters. Eliza, the eldest, was baptised at Dunkeswell on 1 September 1784. At that time Wolford Lodge was still under construction. With the birth of Eliza, Simcoe was even more determined to see it completed and mother and child comfortably settled and with plenty of room for a spacious nursery floor where many little Simcoes would be reared, by servants of course. As was the custom for women of wealth, Elizabeth employed a wet nurse for the little Eliza.

The baptism of Charlotte, the second daughter, took place at Dunkeswell on 3 September 1785, by which time the family had taken up residence in their spacious lodge. Henrietta Maria, always known as Harriet, was baptised on 24 April 1787. Caroline followed on 27 November 1788. Sophia Jemima's date of baptism was 23 October 1789. In all cases the actual date of birth was not set down, a not unusual occurrence in parish records.

For Francis, both dates were recorded. He was born at Wolford Lodge on 6 June 1791, and baptised Francis Gwillim at Dunkeswell on 17 July 1791.[2] His arrival may have given especial satisfaction, but no evidence suggests that the birth of a male heir was any happier an event for either parent than of the five daughters who preceded him. A first son was often named after his paternal grandfather, in this case John the naval captain. Nor was he named for his maternal grandfather, Thomas the colonel. He may have been named, instead, for a close friend of his father's.

Francis Lord Rawdon was a brother-in-arms during the American Revolution. Both men commanded corps of provincial (Loyalist) troops, Simcoe the Queen's Rangers, and Rawdon the Volunteers of Ireland. In 1779, because of their effectiveness, both of these provincial corps were put on a new American establishment and numbered. Simcoe's Rangers became the 1st American Regiment, while the Volunteers of Ireland were constituted the 2nd. Later, Rawdon's corps was also honoured by being placed on the British regular establishment but, he must have had more influence than Simcoe. The Volunteers of Ireland were numbered, the 105th Foot. Lord Rawdon later became the 2nd Earl of Moira (and later still he inherited the title Lord Hastings through his mother). As Lord Moira he wrote many letters pertaining to Francis, and he would become the same mentor to Simcoe's son as Admiral Graves had been to his godson "Graves".

Throughout Francis' life, Great Britain was almost constantly at war with France. The revolution, which began on 14 July 1789 with the storming of the Bastille, the breakdown of authority known as the Reign of Terror, and the rise of Napoleon Bonaparte formed the backdrop to his birth and youth. The evil behaviour of the wicked French was a favourite topic of discussion among the adults of his family and their friends. The French, with their slogans of "liberty, equality and fraternity", were threatening the sanctity of the established order of things. They were setting an appalling example of mob rule that in time provided an opportunity for a bloodthirsty dictator to rampage through Europe. Worse, they had become atheists who had decapitated their divine Monarch and his Queen. The French provided a fine example of the dangers of democracy. They were repeating the nightmare of the sacrilegious execution of Charles I and the horrors of the Commonwealth and Protectorate of Oliver Cromwell. Elizabeth's father's sister who lived at Whitchurch, railed against the writings of Thomas Paine, the possibility of conquest, and praised the necessity of a strong church.

> if we escape a French government we will be happy. If our nation was less dissipated and more religious, I should not fear them. The French Government can not hold together long, because of terrorism.[3]

Some four years before the birth of Francis, Admiral Graves died and Elizabeth's widowed Aunt Margaret moved into Wolford Lodge. The admiral had willed Hembury Fort House to his nephew, Captain Richard Graves, Royal Navy. Her letters, and certain of Mary Anne Burges', show that Margaret felt resentful. As in the case of Elizabeth, upon her marriage the admiral had taken charge of Margaret's fortune, which was considerably larger than his own. She felt that upon his death what was rightfully hers should have been returned to her. Instead, part of her wealth had been willed away to a person who was not even her blood relative.

That Wolford Lodge was so large was a blessing. Aunt Margaret was not the easiest person to accommodate. She could be outspoken, opinionated and argumentative. Accustomed to her, Elizabeth could handle her diplomatically and avoid friction, but Mary Anne Burges admitted, in letters she sent to Canada, that when she first visited Wolford Lodge she had been terrified of the old lady.

Fortunately, Elizabeth's aunt at Whitchurch, Elizabeth Gwillim, was a no-nonsense, down-to-earth person. Her niece referred to her as "Mrs. Gwillim" in her Canadian diary.[4] At that time, a woman who managed her own estate was entitled to use "Mrs." regardless of her marital status. Aunt Elizabeth's letters abound in common sense, probably because she had to make responsible decisions. The Simcoes catered to Aunt Margaret, who incidently was still very wealthy, lest they be dropped from her will.

By the time Francis was born, his father knew that he would be appointed the lieutenant governor of Upper Canada. The old Province of Canada would be divided to accommodate the aspirations of the thousands of American Loyalists who had settled west of the Ottawa River, without interfering with the rights of the French-speaking residents along the lower St. Lawrence. Upper Canada would have English criminal as well as civil law, and freehold land tenure. French civil law and the seigneurial tenure, a form of feudalism, would remain in force in Lower Canada.

The people who would be Simcoe's subjects were living along the shores of the upper St. Lawrence, the Bay of Quinte, at Niagara and Detroit. Nearly all heads of families had served in five Provincial Corps of the British Army and, upon disbandment, had been located in townships assigned to the various regiments. The disbanded provincials had served in the Northern [Military] Department, with headquarters in Quebec City. The regiments of the American establishment, and many other provincial corps had belonged to the Central Department based at New York City. Simcoe's Queen's Rangers had gathered there, and been disbanded in New Brunswick, along with other provincial regiments who were taken from New York by sea in 1783.

Very few of the soldiers, soldiers' wives and soldiers' children who had settled in Upper Canada knew Simcoe personally, but they were prepared to give him a rousing welcome. The disbanded men of Butler's Rangers, the King's Royal Regiment of New York, Loyal Rangers, King's Rangers and Royal Highland Emigrants were kindred spirits. As a man who had led a provincial corps (and succeeded in having it recognized as a British regular regiment) Simcoe already had their respect.

He received permission to raise a new corps, again to be known as the Queen's Rangers, and to wear the same uniform – short green jackets and white gaitered trousers. Most of the recruits and officers were Devon men, but Simcoe confidently expected that some of the veterans settled in New Brunswick would come and re-enlist. Many of Francis Simcoe's earliest memories would be of the garrisons, of bright uniforms, of cannon salutes, of martial music by fife and drum, of bugle calls and drum signals.

The new governor knew that accommodation would be primitive. At a sale of the effects of the late Captain James Cook (who had been the navigator on the *Pembroke* under Captain John Simcoe), the colonel purchased two "canvas houses" that had wooden frames and flooring. These glorified tents could be erected wherever they were needed, then taken down and packed away for future use. He also bought several more conventional tents and large marquees.

Elizabeth gathered together a large wardrobe that befit "The Sovereign Lady of Upper Canada", as Mary Anne Burges dubbed her.[5] When the time came to take their leave of the four little girls who would not be accompanying them, Elizabeth had serious doubts. The soon-to-be governor had no such qualms. Much as he loved his daughters, patriotism, duty to King and Empire, overshadowed every other consideration. He felt confident that the girls would be well looked after by Mrs. Hunt. Nor would Mrs. Hunt neglect education and whatever discipline seemed necessary. As Mary Anne was later to write of Mrs. Hunt, "I know she has as great a satisfaction in taming children, as great Jockeys have in breaking Colts."[6]

The "Gov", (as Elizabeth called him in her diary), with herself, two babes and their nurses left Wolford lodge on 15 September 1791. Family and nurses travelled by carriage; wagons followed, laden with servants, furniture and baggage. They were bound for Weymouth, to embark on His Majesty's frigate *Triton*, twenty-eight guns, Captain G. Murray. They reached Weymouth on the 17th. The *Triton* awaited them, but they could not sail because Simcoe's commission as lieutenant governor had not been signed and was still in London. They had to rent rooms temporarily, while Simcoe fumed over the delay. With every passing day, the danger of finding the St. Lawrence iced over and closed to vessels became more imminent. Finally, they were able to depart on 26 September 1791.

As Baby Francis embarked with family and servants on the *Triton*, he was also embarking upon a mobile, gypsylike existence. His early years would be in contrast to those of his contemporaries.

Chapter 3
Quebec November 1791

The voyage on the *Triton* took forty-eight days, one day short of seven weeks. The Simcoes left Weymouth on a heartening east wind, perfect for the Atlantic crossing. They had started off well, but at that time of the year they knew that some very rough weather was inevitable. By 4 October Elizabeth was quite seasick. "The Children are well but never appear to me safe but when in their Cotts, for the nurses are much indisposed & have very indifferent sea legs." Elsewhere Elizabeth referred to one nurse as "Junk"; the other was Francis' wet nurse, who would be returning to England when he was weaned.

Elizabeth herself was managing to walk on the heaving deck, as long as she had a gentleman's arm for support.

"Sophia's amusement is seeking the Poultry on deck where a little midshipman carries her every day."[1]

The *Triton* sailed southwest for a while. By 10 October the weather was unbearably hot, as they were nearing the Azores, Portuguese territory. The islands were possessions of a country that would have significance in the lives of both the governor and his baby son. Gales on the 15th and 16th deprived everyone of sleep. The ship was very noisy as the rigging creaked constantly, and each roll made a booming sound within. By 20 October the *Triton* was 130 leagues (390 miles) off Newfoundland, in a heavy sea. Gaps in the ship's decking allowed water to drip down, keeping Elizabeth's cabin quite wet. She did not say where the two children and their nurses slept, but probably in their own cabin. On 23 October, Sophia celebrated her second birthday. The confinement at sea was harder on the lively girl than on Francis, who, at six months, was hardly able to crawl.

As days passed, the governor seemed ever more gloomy. He was afraid that the St. Lawrence pilots would have left for the winter, in which event the *Triton* might sail on to Barbados. Elizabeth regretted setting out so late in the year. If they had waited until next spring she would have had that much more time with the four older girls. Then hopes rose when they sighted land birds on the 27th.

They passed Louisbourg on 30 October, where Simcoe longed to stop to see the magnificent harbour his father had described in his papers, records much treasured by his son and grandson. However, time would not permit. After more gales, where the crew's hands were frostbitten from handling ice-covered ropes, they sighted Anticosti. Again the governor gazed keenly about him, wondering where the *Pembroke* had been when Captain John Simcoe died. Now the prevailing wind was against them, but the frigate ploughed steadily on. The pilot came aboard on the 9th, and the *Triton* dropped anchor inside the harbour of Quebec at one a.m. on 11 November.

Francis was scarcely aware of events, but in later years he would devour his mother's account of the voyage, and the details that gave him a sense of reality for his Grandfather Simcoe. Quebec harbour was a dreary sight as dawn rose. Snow turned to rain as the family looked about the new surroundings. At first light the governor left in a ship's boat to meet Major General Alured Clarke, lieutenant governor of Canada then resident in the Château St. Louis, government house. There Simcoe met Prince Edward, Duke of Kent, who was the commander of Thomas Gwillim's onetime regiment. The 7th Royal Fusiliers, in which he had been a major, were the Quebec garrison.

The governor in chief, Guy Carleton 1st Baron Dorchester, General Clarke informed Simcoe, had gone on leave to England. Rumour stated that Dorchester had left at this time because he did not want to greet Simcoe. His Lordship had recommended that Sir John Johnson be appointed to Upper Canada. Johnson was the wealthy baronet from the Mohawk Valley and former commander of the King's Royal Regiment of New York. The government of New York had confiscated thousands of acres that belonged to Sir John. As the most prestigious Loyalist, Dorchester felt that Johnson deserved the honour. He was affronted when the British government disregarded his wish.

Elizabeth, meanwhile, stayed aboard the *Triton*, waiting for the governor to return. The more she looked at dismal, gray Quebec, the more she wanted to remain aboard the *Triton*, which would sail for home as soon as possible. Then Captain Murray joined Elizabeth and introduced Lieutenant Edward Talbot, of the 7th Fusiliers. Talbot had come to the ship bringing a party of soldiers to help the Simcoes. The captain requested that Elizabeth vacate their quarters because passengers were waiting to come aboard, and he was anxious to reach the Atlantic before ice formed downstream in the river. Elizabeth watched as with much efficiency Lieutenant Talbot's men transferred their belongings to a ship's boat and from there to a warehouse in the Lower Town.

On his return from the château, Simcoe informed her that they must rent a house. They could not enter Upper Canada until after the proclamation of the Canada Act, slated for 26 December. As well, many of the men Simcoe had chosen or his council would not arrive until the spring and he could not be sworn in until his Chief Justice, William Osgoode, was on hand. What an inconvenience! As Simcoe well knew, the time to travel most comfortably on land was in winter. Sleighs could negotiate trails and frozen waters with ease. The warmer seasons meant stumps and rutted roads, lack of bridges, stretches of white rapids along waterways, and swarms of stinging insects.

The prospect of winter in Quebec, so distasteful to the governor, left Elizabeth cheerful and undaunted. She quickly recovered from her initial depression, particularly as she was meeting so many welcoming people. They found a house for rent in the Rue St. Jean that led out of the city through the St. Jean Gate. The house was was not large but the only one to be had. In December, after the family was settled in, Simcoe went to Montreal. He returned on the 11th, accompanied by another Lieutenant Talbot, this time Thomas Talbot of the 24th Regiment, as his aide de camp. Talbot would be a good friend to Elizabeth and the children. Among Elizabeth's particular friends were Mme. François Baby and Mme. Ignace de Salaberry. (The latter would lose a son during the Peninsular War.) On Christmas Day, Elizabeth went to the Cathedral with Mme. Baby. The service impressed her, but the wooden building was frightfully cold because fires were forbidden. The winter was the time for social life, when getting about in sleighs was easier than by carriage over roads slippery with melting ice and clogged with mud.

On 13 February she wrote a long letter to Miss Hunt:

Though I anxiously think of & wish to see the Children, I am glad they are not here, as it would be utterly out of my power to have as much of their company as would be necessary. You cannot think what a gay place this is in winter, we do not go to half the amusements we are invited to, & yet there are few days alone;

One item concerned Francis:

I am exceedingly impatient to hear from you whether the Children have the whooping cough, as the Physician here thinks the little Boy has it, but I am fully convinced it is Worms, for which he has just begun to take Medicine & is I hope getting better daily.[2]

Meanwhile, the Simcoes continued making new friends. Among them were the half-pay militia colonel, Henry Caldwell, and his wife Ann neé Hamilton. The colonel had business interests In the city, and a fine country house, Belmont, on the Ste. Foy road that led west out of Quebec. Caldwell, in command of the English militia in 1775 that helped repel the American rebel attack on Quebec, had been in Canada since the Seven Years' War.[3] The colonel had known her father, Thomas Gwillim, at that time, but since Mrs. Simcoe had a different surname, neither spotted the connection.

They had decided not to leave for Upper Canada until May, because they could not go further than Montreal until ships arrived from England with some members of Executive Council and the latest orders for the governor. They were about to move to a better house, after two chimney fires, one of which disrupted a dinner party she was giving in honour of Prince Edward. On 4 March, she recorded the arrival, from New Brunswick, of Aeneas Shaw and eleven others. Shaw had been a captain in the earlier Queen's Rangers, for whom Simcoe was holding a captaincy in the new regiment. Shaw's children would become Francis' friends in Upper Canada.

By that time, the Simcoes were settled into a bigger house whose back rooms overlooked the garden of the Ursuline Convent. By removing a partition upstairs, they created a room forty-five feet long with tea and card rooms adjoining. The 7th Fusiliers were the best dancers, she claimed. Was this a partiality for her father's onetime regiment? She had established a routine, passing the mornings reading and walking with the governor, making time for the children in the afternoons, and attending concerts, plays, suppers and balls in the evenings. "How Happy I am."[4]

The governor did not share her delight. He wanted to get on with his work. He regarded plays as frivolous, and disapproved of young officers acting silly parts. He deplored the lack of intellectual activity, but Elizabeth did not miss it. "I fear you will find me more ignorant when I return than when I set out" she wrote Miss Hunt on 26 April 1792.[5] By that time she was preparing to depart for Upper Canada.

In the same letter she added, "I am so happy that the little Boy has got over the small pox before he sets out." She did not mean that Francis, then ten months old, had contracted the dread disease by accident, but that he had recovered from inoculation. Before Edward Jenner's discovery that people who had had cowpox did not catch smallpox, inoculation was done with matter taken from a patient sick with a mild case of smallpox. If luck held, a healthy person given such an "elective infection" would also have only a mild case, and one that would give immunity. Parents who permitted this type of inoculation were taking a calculated risk, and thus far the Simcoes had been fortunate. On 23 May, Mary Anne Burges wrote that she was anxious to hear from Elizabeth over the effect of inoculation on Francis. She hoped that it was as "serviceable to him as was Caroline's."[6] Sophia must have been inoculated before she left England, for Elizabeth did not mention it in letters that were not included in her diary. Caroline's inoculation may have been postponed owing to an illness.

After receiving Elizabeth's news, Mary Anne responded on 27 July. She was happy to have a good account of "your little Boy." Mrs. Graves had been more disapproving of Francis' inoculation than she was over Caroline's.[7]

The next item in Mary Anne's journal was dated 30 June. Mr. Haynes was a Methodist preacher in Honiton who also kept a school for boys. Mary Anne sometimes took Eliza, Charlotte, Harriet and Caroline with her to chapel, in addition to regular attendance at the parish church in Dunkeswell. Impressed with how well behaved the children were, he enquired what methods Mrs. Simcoe used to make hers so much more amiable than other people's, as he wished to use them on his own little boy.[8] The disciplinarian was, of course, Mrs. Hunt. Before the Simcoes left for Canada, good behaviour was in the hands of the nursery staff. Elizabeth does not mention who they were, but someone warned the children of dire consequences if they misbehaved in front of their mother. Only with Sophia and Francis would Elizabeth find herself confronted by displays of temper and intractability, and not until she was in Upper Canada, coping with inadequate housing that was anything but soundproof.

By June the Simcoes were aware of the French menace. France had declared war on Austria in April, and would soon break the peace with Prussia and Sardinia as well. Many of Simcoe's friends had thought him insane in accepting the appointment to Upper Canada. With war clouds threatening, he would have had endless opportunities for promotion on the battlefields of Europe.

Preparations for the journey to Upper Canada were now nearly complete. Francis' wet nurse had left for England, and Elizabeth had hired an American girl named Collins to accompany them. Three flat-bottomed "bateaux" were waiting alongside a dock that lined the St. Lawrence; the boatmen who would man them were Canadiens. A heat wave struck on 4 June that everyone found utterly debilitating. They had not yet learned to dress for the high temperatures and humidity of summer along the St. Lawrence and the Great Lakes. Simcoe sweated in the woollen breeches and stockings, waistcoat and the red and gold regimental coat of a full colonel in the army, or the green and silver he donned while parading as the commander of the Queen's Rangers. Elizabeth, sweltered in her stays, linen shift and layers of petticoats. For a time she did not believe in allowing Sophia to run about clad only in her linen shift, as other children did, nor that Francis, now beginning to walk and in petticoats, would have been better off without them. Instead she diagnosed him as feverish because his skin was so damp to the touch.

Elizabeth did not make an entry in her diary for 6 June, Francis' first birthday, possibly because she was so busy getting ready to depart. On the 8th the family and servants rose at six a.m., and walked through the St. Louis Gate and downhill to the St. Lawrence. One bateau would carry the governor and his lady, Lieutenant Thomas Talbot, and another aide de camp, Lieutenant Thomas Grey. The second bateau was reserved for Sophia and Francis and nurses Junk and Collins. The other servants and the rest of the baggage rode in the third. Elizabeth's special baggage included a "boydet", or camp chair as large as a mattress, a cot from the *Triton*, and a mosquito net tent to hang over a bed. By the time they set out, Elizabeth knew that Francis' status as the baby would soon end; she was pregnant with her seventh child.

During the bateau journey, the Simcoe party usually rose by six a.m., to allow time for a walk before settling into the not too spacious bateaux. On the 11th they started at four a.m., and went as far as Trois Rivières. They found diverting the nurse Collins' "slow manner, characteristic of the Western States" ... "Being desired to make haste, she replied, 'Must I not put the sugar on the children's breakfast?' in true American tone."[9]

The heat remained excessive, but the evenings were pleasant. The bateau-men "sing incessantly and give a more regular stroke with the oars when accompanied by the tuned." Near Sorel Captain Edward Littlehales, Simcoe's military secretary, overtook them, bringing letters from "you." (Author John Ross Robertson assumed that "you" was Mrs. Hunt, but Elizabeth meant Mary Anne Burges.) Edward Baker Littlehales was Simcoe's right hand man. Then from 1801 to 1820 he was Under-Secretary of the Military Department in Ireland. In Dublin, he would play host to sixteen-year-old Ensign Francis Simcoe.

At Pointe aux Trembles on the Island of Montreal they landed, and went by caleche and wagons to Montreal itself, arriving late on the 16th after a wretched ride over a dreadful road. They stopped for a few days of rest at the Château Ramezay (Government House). After meeting local dignitaries, they set out again, by road, on the 22nd. The bateaumen, meanwhile, had drawn the boats through the Lachine Rapids. They were often offered houses for Elizabeth, nurses and children, while the men usually expected to sleep in the boats. If Elizabeth found a clean house, she accepted; if not she preferred to settle on boxes in the boats or in tents pitched on the shores of the river or on islands.

From the western border of the last French seigneury, the Simcoes received a royal welcome from the disbanded Loyalists and their families. Men donned the green or red coats of their provincial corps and came out in canoes and bateaux to salute the new governor. With some local half-pay officers, Simcoe visited Ile Royale (now Chimney Island, New York, below Prescott, Ontario) to examine the ruins of the French Fort Lévis built during the Seven Years' War. Here he found rusting cannons which he arranged to have moved westward in anticipation of future fortifications he might have to acquire. After passing through the Thousand Islands, which Elizabeth sketched on paper or birch bark, they stopped to inspect a mill on the Gananoque River.

The bateaux entered the harbour at Kingston on Sunday 1 July, where they found a small house awaiting them. The harbour was a sight that even a lad of just one year could appreciate. Here the government's eighty-ton topsail schooners, *Onondaga* and *Mississauga*, and the sloop *Caldwell* rode at anchor, ships that carried troops and provisions to Niagara. Fort Erie and Detroit, with a portage at Fort Chippawa for Lake Erie vessels. To the Simcoes, Lake Ontario seemed like a vast ocean since they could not even see the opposite shore, and the prevailing southwest wind could raise long swells and white-caps.

They went ashore to a warm welcome. More half-pay officers were in their old uniforms. Cannon boomed, joined by musket volleys as Mohawk warriors from their village at Deseronto discharged their weapons. Best of all, drawn up in neat files were the Queen's Rangers. Their rows of small white tents were visible in the background. Francis, wide eyed, stood solemnly beside his father, watching it all while Sophia scampered about when not checked by one of the governor's aides. Consternation reigned when Simcoe announced that his capital would be at Niagara, not Kingston. Lord Dorchester had more or less promised that Kingston would be the capital, but having seen the harbour, which faced the prevailing wind and offered such poor shelter, Simcoe wanted a better anchorage. Besides, Niagara was more central, and as long as British troops garrisoned Fort Niagara, his seat of government would be secure. "Mama" was meeting new friends, among them Elizabeth, the wife of the garrison surgeon, Dr. James Macaulay. Their son, John Simcoe Macaulay, was newly born and a future friend for Francis. On Sunday 8 July, Francis and Sophia stood with their mother and not far from "Papa", resplendent in the red tunic and gold lace of a colonel in the army. Red was more fitting for his role as governor than his green coat as Colonel of the Queen's Rangers. A procession marched towards St. George's Church for the swearing in ceremony. Elizabeth, who did not want to miss the occasion, left the children with their nurses and hurried ahead to the church.

At Kingston the Simcoes acquired their first pet, a small grey and white cat that attached herself to their house. Sophia and Francis were delighted. For Elizabeth, life seemed more normal. Pets abounded in and around Wolford Lodge. They left Kingston on 23 July aboard the schooner *Onondaga*, accommodation Elizabeth described as "tolerable".[10] On the 25th to the children she pointed out the spray rising from the great Falls of Niagara. At the mouth of the Niagara River stood formidable stone Fort Niagara, jutting out on their left. The garrison at the time was the 5th or Northumberland Regiment. Across the river was the tiny town of Niagara (Niagara-on-the-Lake), where the family would live.

For their residence the military had selected Navy Hall, four rundown wooden government buildings, once a headquarters for the Provincial Marine on the lake. Workmen had not completed converting these warehouses into a dwelling. Neither Elizabeth nor the governor was enchanted with their future home. To Mary Anne's brother, James Bland Burges, Simcoe wrote, "I am fitting up an old hovel, that will look exactly like a carrier's ale-house in England when properly decorated and ornamented."[11]

Simcoe ordered three tents erected as temporary shelter, one for himself and Elizabeth, one for the children and nurses, and the third for the other servants. They were placed on a hillside, where the view was splendid. Above them rose the steep escarpment. The Queen's Rangers' tents stood at Queenston, the lower landing below the escarpment over which the waters from

Lake Erie tumbled. forming Niagara Falls. Out of sight was the upper landing, at Chippawa. A portage road up the escarpment linked the two landings. The site where the tents stood caught the breeze and was cooler than around low lying Navy Hall. The campsite made a fine place for Sophia to run about and turn somersaults pursued as best he could by Francis. He lumbered along on chubby legs that were still shorter than his torso. Their nurses kept watchful eyes. Mrs. Simcoe had an unholy dread of rattlesnakes which she expected to find everywhere, just waiting to attack.

The children soon had a second pet. An overgrown puppy Elizabeth thought must be some type of hound adopted them, and the governor named him Trojan. Cat and dog provided endless amusement for the growing children. Their mother arranged for meals to be served in a cool "bower", rather than in an airless tent. Sophia, now nearly three, had learned to say "No!", and to struggle when her demands met with disapproval. Francis, still delighted to be walking about and too busy exploring his world, was deemed the better natured child.

Chapter 4

Newark 1792-1793

B y August the Simcoes knew that they would be hosts to Prince
Edward Duke of Kent (and father of Queen Victoria). The prince was
the first Royal to visit Upper Canada. Elizabeth was deeply
depressed. Navy Hall was still unfinished, and the two canvas houses which
Simcoe had purchased from Captain James Cook's belongings had not yet
arrived from Quebec. The governor decided that the prince must have their
tents, while the family would make do with Navy Hall. The place smelt of a
combination of musty damp and new paint. In later letters Elizabeth said how
nauseating new paint was, and how long a room was unfit for use until the
odour had subsided.

The prince's visit began on 20 August. Although he occupied the tents, the
family continued to take their meals in the bower. Elizabeth described it as
made of oak branches. On the 22nd, Simcoe found time to write to Charlotte,
who had celebrated her seventh birthday four days earlier:

> My dear Charlotte, here I am & Mama sitting in a very large bower,
> fronting upon a very fine River, & as high above it, as the sand cliff
> above the Shrubbery, with Sophia sitting upon the Table, little Francis
> with his bald Pole [poll, meaning head] laughing & eating Bilberries.

He wondered whether he should learn to play the fiddle so that he could
accompany Charlotte, who so loved to dance. He was glad Charlotte was
learning to love reading. All four sisters should make Francis fond of it, too,
and not destroy too many birds, sail his little boats and fire his cannon "as
Boys are apt to do."[1]

To Eliza he wrote of his love of Plutarch's Lives, and of how pleased he
was to learn that she was reading the book, for "it will be necessary for Francis
to know them by heart."[2]

Unlike Mama in her diary, when he wrote to the girls at Wolford Lodge,
Papa was not concerned about offending their sensibilities. He thought details
about the lives of Francis and Sophia in Canada were important. Their sisters

had a right to know about their daily doings, so that they could share the experience and imagine they were really there.

The following day, accompanying the prince on an inspection of Fort Niagara and its garrison, the governor stood very close to a cannon during the salute. Even when his hearing returned, he had such a fearful pain in his head that he had to retire to his bed. For a fortnight he remained there, in chilly, inhospitable Navy Hall. Later evidence would suggest that part of the governor's problem was the atmosphere in Navy Hall. He apparently suffered from asthma, caused by both the new paint and moulds. As soon as the prince left, Elizabeth and the children returned to the tents, although the weather had turned unusually cold.

The next important event was the opening of the first legislature, in the Masonic Lodge, where church services were also held. In preparation, Simcoe bestowed a proper English name on his fledgling capital. It would be Newark; Niagara was an outlandish aboriginal name, quite undignified. Elections during the summer had chosen the Members of Parliament. On 16 September Simcoe rode forth in his full scarlet regimentals, escorted by Edward Littlehales, now a Major, Lieutenants Talbot and Grey. The Queen's Rangers and some of Colonel John Butler's disbanded Rangers, both in their green coats, formed the guard of honour along the route from Navy Hall to the Masonic Lodge. Francis and Sophia stood with their mother, proudly watching Papa, already aware that he was the most important person at Newark.

While the legislature was still in session, the canvas houses arrived. The Queen's Rangers were busy erecting "huts" to occupy during the winter, but a work party was detached to erect one of the houses. It was for Elizabeth's use, as her pregnancy was now well advanced. She described it on 28 November:

> The partition was put in the Canvas House today by which means I have a bedroom in it as well as a sitting room. These Houses are very comfortable about 30 feet long. The grates did not answer for burning wood & I have had a Stove placed instead tho as yet a fire has not been wanted. The weather is so mild that we have walked in the Garden from 8 til 9 in the Moon light these two last Evenings.[3]

She did not mention how the second canvas house was used, perhaps for the nurses and children, or an office for the governor. Nor did Elizabeth tell what use the family made of Navy Hall beyond saying that her canvas house was separate from the rest of the house and quiet. The canvas houses were considerably more elaborate than large tents. The floor of hers was of boards, as were the sides, which were wallpapered. Boards placed on the canvas roof kept out the wind. One visitor who met with Governor Simcoe recalled hearing children crying in the next room, but he did not specify whether he was in a canvas house or Navy Hall.

On 9 December Captain Joseph Brant, the Mohawk war leader, dined with the Simcoes. Elizabeth suspected him of cunning, but to Francis he was intriguingly exotic. As he grew older, Francis took great delight in greeting the natives. "He shakes hands in a very friendly manner, tho he is very shy & ungracious to all his own Countrymen.[4] (Since his mother felt the same way, he may have had an example to follow.)

The following day the governor left with some of his staff to walk to Burlington Bay, some fifty miles away along the lakeshore. He returned on the 17th, having turned back two days before. The Simcoes now had a new pet, a Newfoundland dog the governor named Jack Sharp. The children gave him a royal welcome. Trojan, who had grown tired of being mauled, had decided Elizabeth was his mistress. He had taken to sleeping in her room.

By 23 December Trojan was in disgrace. That afternoon, while Elizabeth was at dinner, the hound had chewed up a map of Canada and the United States, "which I had taken great pains to draw. I must paste it together again but its appearance is spoiled. The Gov. made some very pretty Verses on the occasion."[5] As Francis would soon discover, his father wrote atrocious poetry, to amuse his friends, always on a patriotic theme. "Upon the Dog Trojan tearing the Map of N. America" begins:

High thro' the lurid air of heav'n
The haggard vulture spread its pinion
Making that spreme dominion
To the Woman Chief was givn.
With dauntless mind & daring aim
Upwards bold Romulus his eyebeams threw
"Mine is the Augasy, the martial claim
"And Mine the steps of Empire to pursue.[6]

They must have contrasted the isolation and the small scale parties with the grand festivities Simcoe liked to stage at Wolford Lodge. For these he wrote plays, or adaptations of the classics for the children and their friends to perform. Had they been living at Wolford Lodge in 1792, the older girls would have been rehearsing for weeks, while Elizabeth supervised the making of costumes. The big house was always crowded with guests, some of them neighbours, others staying. She did not say how they passed the day, but as her time of "confinement" was so close, she stayed home while the governor attended celebrations. During the day he took the children along because women in particular enjoyed making a fuss over them.

On 16 January 1793, in the canvas house, Elizabeth gave birth to another daughter, named Katherine after Simcoe's mother. In a letter to Mrs. Hunt dated February 1793, she wrote, "Francis is the most engaging pretty child you ever saw of his age; he is at present very handsome." Elizabeth deplored the lack of a wet nurse for the baby.[7] Although she thought little Katherine was growing fat, she did not say what she was being fed. Mare's milk was used if it was available, as it had a lower fat content and was more easily digested than cow's or goat's milk. Elizabeth did not mention the birth in the diary, but an elated Mary Anne Burges described how the girls at Wolford Lodge received the news:

> They are all consulting which of them the new sister is to belong to, & have allotted her to Caroline, who is more vain on the occasion than you can imagine. Harriet said she would give the baby such and such out of her own garden, & Caroline gave her a curtsy & said, "Thank you, Harriet for making presents to my child Katherine." Charlotte likewise is very bountiful to her.[8]

She also had news to relay about Mrs. Margaret Graves. Elizabeth's aunt had moved out of Wolford Lodge, taking her possessions along. She had purchased a terrace house in Lansdown Crescent, Bath. On 13 March 1893, Elizabeth wrote to Mrs Hunt that she was not surprised. "I thought such an event not improbable."[9]

Mary Anne wrote again on 15 June 1793, enquiring after both Katherine and Francis. "Tell me who she [Katherine] is like & how she gets on because I consider her a future friend." She was delighted to hear that Francis was turning into such a fine boy, because she had predicted, "a very extraordinary personage, for if he were not it would be proof he was changed in his cradle." She was not at all afraid of his being spoilt. In closing she added that she was always sorry to finish a letter, for it seemed as though her conversation with Elizabeth had ended.[10]

In a letter written 20 November 1792, which did not reach Elizabeth until the spring, Mary Anne was:

> Sorry Sophia is so tiresome but that is her age when all children are so self-willed & unpleasant. She will soon grow out of it as the rest have, I had no idea a child of yours could be disagreeable.... Most children make struggle for independence but when they find they must submit do so with a good grace & the trouble is over."[11]

The news from Europe was grim. On 21 January the French had sent deposed King Louis XVI to the guillotine, shameful deed! On 1 February France declared war on Britain and Holland, and on the 13th Britain, Austria, Prussia, Holland, Spain and Sardinia formed a coalition against France. On 7 March France declared war against Spain. No one at Niagara/Newark could forget that the United States was France's ally, ever since the French had sent troops to aid the rebelling Americans against the British. On 22 April, the

United States declared itself neutral. The Americans would not attack Canada to aid the French, but Simcoe wanted his garrison reinforced. The Americans might attack if they thought their own interests were at stake. While the governor was aware of the role he might be playing back home as the British army mobilized, he still felt he had vital work to do to protect Upper Canada and to provide wise leadership.

Meanwhile, Elizabeth was grieving the loss of the map-chewing Trojan. A sudden heat wave had struck, the thermometer registering 112 "Fahrenheit" in the sun at Navy Hall. Trojan, ill because of a blow on his head, had run into the water. Servants, convinced he was mad, had shot him. Sophia and Francis, too, were upset. Even though Trojan often escaped from them to Mama, Jack Sharp was Papa's dog and not as fine a plaything.

Late in April, Captain Aeneas Shaw, who had joined Simcoe at Quebec after marching on snowshoes from New Brunswick, arrived at Newark from Oswego. With him were Mrs. Shaw and their seven children, brought overland from New Brunswick. They had reached Oswego the previous autumn and wintered in a cabin near the fort, where Captain Shaw met them. Officially, Fort Oswego was in New York State but, like Fort Niagara, it was still in British hands. "The South Shore of Lake Ontario being uninhabited, from Oswego they brought with them an Indian to build Hutts & shoot Partridges & Ducks. They came the whole way in a Boat."[12]

In May, the governor left by boat with seven officers to explore the Toronto Carrying Place. Lord Dorchester, back in Quebec after his leave, ordered Simcoe to build a naval base there, as it was the best harbour on the Canadian side of Lake Ontario. The governor returned on the 13th, very pleased with the harbour. If the Americans could force the British garrison to leave Fort Niagara, Simcoe would have a temporary capital there.

The Shaw children were a happy addition to Newark, and only too pleased to let Francis trail after them while keeping him out of danger. His second birthday, on 6 June, was more noteworthy than his first, now that he was so much more a real person. Elizabeth did not mention the event in her diary; at the time she had a severe cold and was at Fort Niagara. In search of a change of air, she had accepted an invitation from the wife of the commandant, Major John Smith, to convalesce in her quarters. She did not return to Navy Hall until the 14th.

By 5 July, Francis was ill, because of the extreme heat around Navy Hall. The Simcoes decided that Elizabeth should take Francis and Sophia to camp up in the mountain where the cool breezes blew.

> I shall have an establishment of Two marquees a Tent & two sentrys. The Gov. will come to see us whenever he had leisure, my dinner to be sent every day from Navy Hall. This day I embarked at one o'clock on board the Gun boat with Francis & Sophia & Mr. Mayne attended me.

Their escort was Captain William Mayne, of the Queen's Rangers, who was a Devon man. They did not reach the camp until five p.m. They made poor headway because the current in the Niagara River ran at four knots an hour. "The Gun Boat not having top sails catches but little wind between the high banks."[13]

They did find the camp more comfortable than Newark. Elizabeth had been befriended by Catherine Askin, wife of a well-to-do merchant, Robert Hamilton, who had built a fine stone house at Queenston. On 9 July Elizabeth was entertaining Mrs. Hamilton, and her sister, Madeline, wife of Dr. John Richardson, a military surgeon. Catherine and Madeline were daughters of a fur trader at Detroit and a French mother, convent-educated, cultured women. They were in Elizabeth's "Arbour" when a sudden thunderstorm interrupted them and everyone sought shelter in the tents. Afterward, "Mrs. Hamilton took Francis home with her lest he should catch cold from the Damp of the Tents after this violent rain. I drank tea & slept at Mrs. Hamilton's."

Sophia, apparently, was less prone to colds. Also, where was baby Katherine? Had she been left with one of the nurses at Navy Hall? By the 23rd, the weather still very hot, Francis was much better but weak. "I see him almost every day but did not chuse to pay Mrs. Hamilton so long a visit tho I feel greatly obliged to her for keeping the child."[14]

Leaving Francis for two long weeks with Mrs. Hamilton seems like an imposition. It may have been, but well-to-do people were much accustomed to visits for weeks or months. Elizabeth would have sent one of the nurses with Francis to do the work of caring for him. Mrs. Hamilton merely provided the house.

Mary Anne Burges wrote of paying a visit to Mrs. Graves' home in Bath that lasted long after she wished to return home to Tracey. She soon found she could pay no attention to Mrs. Graves' mood swings and capriciousness. Her hostess was so anxious to have her stay longer that she tried to be less argumentative. Mary Anne added that Mrs. Graves had the welfare of Francis at heart more than she would care to admit. She relayed news of him, sometimes with "the appearance of superstition."[15]

Mrs. Graves also wished to have her favourite great niece, Eliza, come for extended visits. In her letter to Mrs. Hunt of 13 March 1793, Elizabeth explained why she did not want prolonged visits:

As for Mrs. Graves' desire of having Eliza on a visit, we cannot refuse it; but it is Coll. Simcoe's & my absolute desire that she does not stay above a month or six weeks in these annual visits, because we should be sorry the child's education should be stopped or that she should be longer separated from her sisters, which reasons alone determined us to deprive ourselves of her company... The other Children, of course, Mrs. G. would not wish to be troubled with; if she did the same system should prevail as with regard to Eliza.[16]

Between the lines was the Simcoes' joint wish to avoid giving offense to such a wealthy relation. A month to six weeks was a long time for Eliza's education to be neglected, but Elizabeth did not find the length of the proposed visit unusual. (How often did the hosts in Jane Austen's novels entreat guests to stay on for another month or so?)

Now that Francis was recovered, Elizabeth felt obliged to break camp and return to Navy Hall. Plans were well under way for the Simcoes to move to Toronto, which the governor wanted ready in case he had to move his government there. Captain Shaw had left Newark on 20 July with 100 men, in bateaux, a working party to begin establishing a town. Simcoe wanted a townsite laid out, on a grid plan, and land cleared for a fort and garrison at the entrance to the harbour. The sheltered water had been created by the silting up of a large sandbar, behind which was some deep water, and some swamp. A

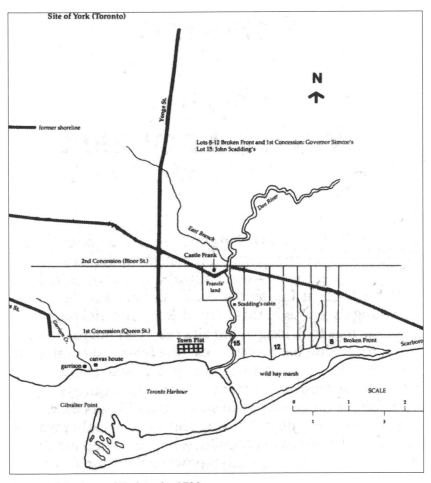

Town and Harbour of York in the 1790s.

blockhouse on the end of the sandspit would guard the harbour. Simcoe named it Gibraltar Point. The Garrison would be opposite it, and the town laid out some two miles to the east where it would be less vulnerable to attack.

  Elizabeth was looking forward to the move. The climate might be better for the children, especially the delicate Francis. Accommodation might be confined to the canvas houses, but they would surely be no more uncomfortable than at Navy Hall. By 29 July, they were ready to sail for Toronto, to begin a new phase of their stay in Upper Canada. All the Simcoes had made friends, but most would also be moving from Newark to join them.

Chapter 5
War Clouds

E ven for the children, the departure, aboard the *Mississauga* was festive. The band of the Queen's Rangers was playing. The Queen's Rangers had a "band of music", the gift of the Simcoes' friend, the Marquis of Buckingham.[1] Regiments had fifes, drums and bugles as military instruments and for signalling. Simcoe could draw regimental funds to pay for the latter, but the the officers, chiefly the Colonel himself, paid the wages to the members of the band of music.

When the children awoke, on Tuesday 30 July, it was daylight. The schooner lay off the long sandbar their mother would call the Peninsula. Eager to miss nothing, Sophia and Francis were asking when they could go ashore. They were waiting, Papa explained, for a Monsieur Rousseau, to come aboard as the pilot. The captain of the *Mississauga* did not know the waters of the harbour. Soon Jean Baptiste Rousseau arrived in a small boat and took over the wheel. He was a French-speaking fur trader with a house at the mouth of the soon-to-be-named Humber River. After dinner, about mid-afternoon, the governor and Elizabeth went ashore taking the dog Jack Sharp. The children must wait until there was a proper place to put them. Meanwhile, they could gaze upon the Queen's Rangers' small white tents, in their neat rows, and on the activity along the waterfront or, when tired of looking, run around the deck or up and down the companionway that led to the cabins and the hold. At night their parents returned to the *Mississauga* to sleep.

Not until 5 August was one of the canvas houses erected for their use. It stood on a rise, separated from the Rangers' encampment by a small creek. Elizabeth hoped that Toronto would be a healthier place than Newark, a spot where Francis would have fewer fevers and other complaints. At the time Lieutenant Talbot was on a mission for the governor to Philadelphia, at the time the capital of the United States. The other aide, Lieutenant Grey was on an errand to Quebec. In their absence, Captain William Mayne, of the Queen's Rangers, acted as an aide and a companion to Elizabeth and the children.

By 24 August, parents and children were as comfortably settled in the canvas house as it allowed. Other tents accommodated baby Katherine and the nurses, the servants and extra furniture and baggage. That day Simcoe received an official account of the Duke of York's success and at once disposed of another outlandish name. The Duke:

> having distinguished himself at Famars by which the French were dislodged & driven out of Holland. The Gov. ordered a Royal Salute to be fired in commemoration of this Event & took the same opportunity of naming this station York. There are a few 12 & 18 Pounders which were brought here from Oswegatchie [the fort on the site of Ogdensburg, New York] & Carleton Island. The Mississauga & Onondaga fired also & the Regt.[2]

Present at the celebration was a party of Ojibwa natives who seemed to appreciate the noise. "One of them named Canise took Francis in his arms & was much pleased to find the Child not afraid but delighted with the sound." To this report, Mary Anne Burges replied:

> Francis displayed great intrepidity by standing by the cannon, an incident which may be related in a history of his life if he proves to be as great a man as I chase he should be.[3]

The performance of Prince Frederick Augustus Duke of York was not quite as glorious as Elizabeth understood it. He had captured the northern French town of Valenciennes on 26 July. The French retook it on 6 September and then forced the Duke to abandon his siege of Dunkirk.

By 23 September they were dining in a marquee because the weather had turned too cold for the arbour. The second canvas house, the governor had decided, would be erected as a winter dining room. The Queen's Rangers were again building huts for winter shelter, and planning a blockhouse, on the site of the present Fort York. Simcoe next led a party to Lake Huron. During the return march, native guides lost the way, so that the men were out of food and they knew not how far from York. They were on the point of consuming Jack Sharp, Simcoe related, when, from a rise they could see the lake. The thought of the men eating the dog horrified the children. Even Jack Sharp was better than no dog at all, but they could not help laughing when Papa described how ungainly the big dog was in a canoe.

Simcoe next selected a 200-acre lot and put it in Francis' name. The tract was delightfully situated on a promontory high above the valley of the Don, as they had called the river that flowed into the swamp at the eastern end of the harbour. By law, to secure Francis' title to the land, they had to build a house within a year. On Tuesday, 29 October the Simcoe family, with required aides and servants, set off to choose the right place:

We went 6 miles by water & landed, climbed up an exceeding steep hill
or rather a series of sugar-loafed Hills & approved of the highest spot
from whence we looked down on the tops of Large Trees & seeing
Eagles near I suppose they build here. There are large Pine plains around
it which being without underwood I can ride or walk on, & we hope the
height of the situation will secure us from Musquitos [sic]. We dined by
a large fire on wild ducks & Chowder on the side of a hill opposite to that
spot.[4]

Elizabeth's mention of the land being "without underwood" meant virgin
forest; tangles of underbrush signified second growth timber. They decided to
name the house Castle Frank, the only place where the nickname was written;
everywhere else all the family used Francis' full name.

Francis was also learning politeness. On 2 December, when one Great
Sail brought his wife and ten children to meet the Simcoes, his mother had him
hand out plates of apples to the native guests.

By the end of December, Thomas Talbot, now a captain, was skating on
the frozen bay. He would soon be leaving York, to return to the 24th Regiment,
his tour of duty as Simcoe's aide at an end. Elizabeth and the children would
miss his friendly company very much. On the 29th, Mary Anne Burges was
writing, "You cannot think what a fancy I have to see Francis. I am uncommonly glad that he deserved such an account as you give of him. Is Katherine
like any of the rest?"[5]

On 1 January 1794, she noted, if the Simcoes were in England, the governor would be "employed against these villainous Frenchmen and tormented by
Mrs. Graves ... she has a particular art of tormenting people who are anxious
for the safety of others."[6]

Certainly French behaviour was an aberration to everything the Simcoes
valued. The French reign of terror had begun in June, and Mme. la Guillotine
was rarely still. On 5 October the French abolished Christianity, and on the
16th former Queen Marie Antoinette was executed. A young Corsican named
Napoleon Bonaparte was now a brigadier general in the French Army. On the
home front, Governor Simcoe had persuaded his legislature to phase out slav-
ery. No more slaves could be brought into Upper Canada; children born to
slaves would be free at age twenty-five.

On 16 January Katherine Simcoe celebrated her first birthday, an event
not mentioned in the diary. The weather soon grew very cold, but snowfalls
had been light, which Elizabeth thought had made deer difficult to track. Hungry native women and children came often to the windows for bread, "which
we cannot refuse them, tho having but a certain quantity of flour until the
Spring arrives, it is inconvenient to give them what they require."[7] Francis was
learning by example. Soon, when he encountered natives, he was quick to find
some food to offer them.

By late March the governor had set off with a work party for Detroit. On the 15th he received an order from Lord Dorchester to erect a fort on the "Miami" [Maumee] River, as an outpost to protect Detroit. Officially, both Fort Niagara and Detroit, although occupied by British garrisons, were on United States territory. Establishing another post on American soil was, Simcoe believed, provocative. He had no option but to obey. No matter how much Simcoe disliked the situation, Dorchester was his superior officer and the military governor of both provinces.

On 14 April Mary Anne wrote that if she had drawn a horoscope for Francis, she "would have passed for a very wonderful Astrologer". Everything Elizabeth had written about him agreed with Mary Anne's notion of him.[8] Sometimes parts of her letters were in Spanish, and she would open with "Mi mas querida amiga". As young girls, she and Elizabeth had studied Spanish together, and both liked to read novels in that language.

Governor Simcoe was still away on his mission to Detroit and the Maumee when Elizabeth had to face her greatest sorrow to date. On 19 April, baby Katherine died. In a letter dated "York May 1794" she wrote to Mrs. Hunt:

> It is with pain I take up my pen to inform you of the loss we have sustained & the melancholy event of our losing poor little Katherine, one of the strongest healthiest children you ever saw ... She had been feverish one or two days cutting teeth, which not being an unusual case with children I was not much alarmed. On good Friday she was playing in my room in the morning, in the afternoon was seized with fits. I sat up the whole night the greatest part of which she continued to have spasms & before morning she was no more.[9]

Elizabeth blamed the death on the absence of James Macaulay, their regular doctor. The attending surgeon she thought less capable. Katherine was the sweetest tempered child imaginable, just beginning to talk and walk, "& the suddenness of the event you may be sure shocked me inexpressibly." A few days later Francis was slightly unwell, but so upset was Elizabeth that she sent "express for our own Surgeon". She continued, "the loss of so promising a Child must long be a painful thing." To make matters even more melancholy, the governor was far away. Two weeks later, when he reached Fort Erie, he heard that Katherine was dead and Elizabeth herself was not expected to live. He rode the eighteen miles to Niagara in two hours. There he learned that Elizabeth was not so much ill as depressed but he still kept up the fast pace so that he could comfort her.

Towards the end of her letter to Mrs. Hunt, Elizabeth was making an effort to sound more positive. "Francis is in perfect health, he has exactly Eliza's affectionate temper & the meekest little thing imaginable, tho a stout fine looking boy." Was Francis truly meek or merely astute enough to avoid the kind of rows Sophia could stir up?

Katherine was laid to rest in the military cemetery at Fort York. The following year, a small marble tombstone sent from Honiton was placed on the grave. It read "Katherine Simcoe, January 16, 1793 - April 19, 1794. Happy in the Lord."

At the time of the death, Sophia, nearly four and a half years old, was as sorrowing as her parents. Francis, at nearly three, knew that something was missing, but he could not understand why. Elizabeth believed that Katherine had been a healthy child, but she could have been wrong. The cause of death might have been the long-term result of not receiving mother's milk as an infant. Breast feeding would have given her a stronger immune system.

When Mrs. Elizabeth Gwillim, Elizabeth's aunt at Whitchurch, heard of Katherine's death, she wrote to Eliza Simcoe, now over ten years old. Her great aunt's common sense approach must have been hurtful to a child who had lost a sister she would never see. Mrs. Gwillim was sorry to hear in a letter from Mama of the loss of Eliza's little sister, but thankful that so many more were left. "All who die in infance go to heaven." She closed with, "I hear your brother wears Indian dress that is more becoming than English on the young."[10] Did she know how natives dressed from viewing Elizabeth's sketches?

By May the governor had decided to return to Niagara for the summer session of the legislature because York had little suitable accommodation. At Newark the legislature could meet in a "Council Chamber". This was probably an addition to Butler's Barracks, which stood on the military reserve where Fort George was under construction. They left York on the 9th in an open boat along the shore. Simcoe wanted to inspect the land as they went. The children enjoyed this journey. Although they had to sit still, they had time to run about during frequent stops. On the 10th they walked with their mother half a mile to a farmhouse where they bought fresh bread and milk. After they returned to camp for the night, "Francis lay down on his Great Coat & slept until the tent was ready for him."

They reached Newark at noon on the 11th, the latter part of the trip unpleasant in wind and rain. People at Newark were tense. In Philadelphia the United States government was accusing the British of helping the natives in the northwest. Simcoe feared that a renewed alliance with France would mean an attack on vulnerable Upper Canada. If the Americans threatened the upper province, Elizabeth would take the children to Quebec.

Daily the governor went to Fort Niagara to confer with the officers of the garrison. Sometimes Elizabeth and the children and went in the boat with him and took walks on the military reserve. On 3 June, Simcoe was so late with the commanding engineer that darkness descended. Francis fell asleep on the "Common" before the governor was ready to leave. His third birthday fell on 6

June, but they did not celebrate it until the 7th because Simcoe was away inspecting Fort Chippawa. A welcome gift was a miniature cannon from Mr. John Macdonell, a half-pay captain from Butler's Rangers, a member for Glengarry, and speaker of the Legislative Assembly:

> Today the little Cannon Mr. McDonell [sic] gave him fired a salute of 21 guns & though they are not 2 inches long made a loud Report & pleased him much. Being 3 years old he was dressed in a Rifle shirt & sash, which gave him somewhat the air of an Indian.[11]

By age three, like most boys, Francis was reliable and no longer in petticoats. A rifle shirt was usually dark green, and fringed, the sash brightly coloured. The rest of his attire could have been mid-calf trousers or breeches, with coloured stockings and moccasins. Was this what Mrs. Gwillim thought of as Indian dress? Three days later some men of the Seneca nation arrived and performed war dances to a chant. Afterwards Francis "imitated their dancing & singing surprisingly well."

On Saturday 26 July, Elizabeth and Francis set off with Captain Mayne to explore the shore once more. They slept in a house that belonged to Colonel John Butler. The next morning Francis had a cold, and they left him with a servant while they continued a far as Forty Mile Creek, which Elizabeth wanted to visit. At a farm where they called for provisions, a woman advised Elizabeth to treat Francis with a plant called crow's foot. Boiled in milk until it became red and thick, it would cure the complaint in his stomach. Reunited with Francis, she followed this advice, which helped him. They were back in Newark by the 29th. Sophia had not been on the journey. As she was now aged four years, nine months, Elizabeth had found someone to give her lessons, or who kept a school for children of families who could pay for tutoring.

By 12 August, the Simcoes had decided that Elizabeth would definitely be leaving for Quebec. "An express from Detroit. It is now decided that I am to go to Quebec next month. The hostile appearance Mr. Wayne's conduct bears makes the continuance of Peace with the U. States very doubtful." (Mr. Wayne, was General "Mad Anthony", then leading American troops against the natives. He defeated them at Fallen Timbers, Maumee River, on 20 August 1794.)

Elizabeth wrote to her friend, Ann Caldwell, asking her to rent a house:

> Should the French & Americans assault Quebec this winter, I shall find more comfort in Mrs. Caldwell's society than in that of most others, as such a scene would not be new to her. She was in the town when besieged by Montgomery, 1775. Coll. Caldwell was one of the most active defenders of it.[12]

Colonel Henry Caldwell had been in command of the British (English-speaking) Militia during the attack on Quebec by Richard Montgomery and Benedict Arnold. (Montgomery was killed. Arnold withdrew to Montreal until the spring of 1776 when fresh reinforcements from Britain forced the Americans to abandon their occupation of Canada.)

At Newark, war fever mounted. Captain David Shank, of the Queen's Rangers, arrived with a detachment from York for the Maumee "Miamis" and Captain John McGill soon followed with more Rangers. On 12 September Simcoe finally left for Detroit. On the 13th Elizabeth and the children sailed on the *Mississauga* for Kingston. She mentioned only Collins as accompanying her, but Junk may have been along, too. Captain John McGill was their escort, to smooth the way by hiring bateaux and finding sleeping accommodation.

Although people in her party were supposed to be the only passengers, Elizabeth agreed to allow Molly, sister of Captain Joseph Brant, to come along. Molly Brant was the widow of Sir William Johnson, Superintendent of the Indian Department until his death in 1774. Detractors in the Mohawk Valley referred to her as "Brown Lady Johnson". She never took her husband's name because she preferred to retain her status as one of the clan matrons who made important decisions for the Mohawks. She had a house in Kingston, a reward for the Brants' work that kept their people on the side of the British during the American Revolution.

The crossing was very rough. The *Mississauga* anchored in Kingston harbour on the morning of 15 September. Captain McGill found one government bateau and hired another from a merchant. As on the upbound journey of spring 1792, the men slept in the boats, while Elizabeth, children and Collins were in houses, if they met with her approval. On Lake St. Francis a storm threatened and Captain McGill suggested heading for shore. Elizabeth wanted to push on, to her regret. The wind and waves were particularly violent, rain sifted down. The children were crying and Collins kept sighing. Elizabeth feared that they would be blown into American waters, but Captain McGill cajoled the boatmen to greater efforts with offers of rum. They made shore. At an inn, the Adjutant-General of Militia, Hugh Macdonell, had taken a room which he surrendered to Elizabeth. The room had very large fires where they were able to dry out and sleep well.

As on the journey west, the roads as they neared Montreal were impossible. On 18 September, they had to wait two hours for a "Calesh" (caleche) before Elizabeth could set out with Francis. She hired:

> A Carriage so indifferent that I was obliged to stop & take Collins with me to hold the Child or we should have been shaken out. I was so fatigued with this ten miles to Montreal that I determined never to go in a Post Calesh again. The carriage was driven tandem the first horse tied to

the other by a rope which not in the least confine him. The horses generally went different ways & at a great rate.[13]

She did not reveal where Sophia was, nor the whereabouts of Collins
before she needed help with Francis. This extract, and many others where
Sophia seems not to exist, were inserts to the diary from letters Elizabeth had
written to Mary Anne Burges.

Elizabeth and her entourage stayed three nights at the home of Joseph
Frobisher, a wealthy fur trader. They were on their way in the bateaux on the
21st, a Sunday. On the 24th they were about four miles from Belmont, the
home of Colonel and Mrs. Caldwell. They left most of their baggage on the
boats, with servants, taking only what they would need for a few days. Elizabeth stopped at a Post House to change out of her travelling clothes. Despite
her earlier vow they took a caleche the rest of the way, to a friendly reception.

Chapter 6
Quebec and Return to York

They stayed for a few days at Belmont, until Elizabeth could find a house she liked. Many friends came to call, among them Ann, a daughter of Sir John Johnson whom Elizabeth found congenial. On 12 October, Colonel George Beckwith was among the dinner guests. From a casual remark, Elizabeth discovered that Colonel Caldwell had known her father during the Seven Years' War when both officers had served under Wolfe. Colonel Caldwell was astonished that he had known Mrs. Simcoe since the autumn of 1791, but had never dreamed that she was the daughter of Thomas Gwillim. In fact, he had stayed in the Gwillim house in London following the death of General Wolfe.

On the 14th, Elizabeth took possession of a house in Palace Street. She had found a school for Sophia, which she thought would provide the discipline she failed to impose. Her time was filled with entertaining and visiting with old friends like Mme Baby and now with Miss Ann Johnson. Francis usually accompanied her during the day and became her most constant companion. She was soon invited to tea at the Château St. Louis, Government House. Lady Dorchester was kindness itself to Elizabeth and the children, even though Simcoe and Lord Dorchester rarely saw eye to eye.[1]

By 8 November, the war scare was receding. Simcoe wrote to Charlotte from Newark. He explained that he had felt obliged to send Mama, Francis and Sophia to Quebec because of the talk of war, and he had made ready his great sword and the big grey horse. Now he was to set out for York, and go all round the lake to Kingston:

> to meet Mama & Sophia & the little dog Francis. He thought himself so fine in his red stockings or Legings [sic] & Indian cloak, that he acts as if he was twenty years old, but he is good natured.[2]

Simcoe proposed meeting the family at Pointe au Baudet, on the border between Upper and Lower Canada, in January or February when the ice would be strong and travelling a pleasure. Elizabeth was already enjoying drives through Quebec in a carriole, or open sleigh, which Lady Dorchester had loaned her. She was finding both Dorchesters "uniformly polite & obliging to me".

Now that Francis and Sophia wanted to be active out of doors, Elizabeth found warmer winter attire for them than English greatcoats or Indian blankets. She ordered coats long enough to reach their ankles, with room for growth, made of thick blankets, the colour of natural wool, but with wide stripes of red. With them went tuques and sashes of brightly coloured wool, mittens to cover their gloves, and fur-lined moccasins.

The Christmas festivities, which went on non-stop, were spoiled by the illness of Francis. Elizabeth sat up with him on the nights of 20 to 24 December. Dr. Nooth, who was called to see Francis, could not decide whether he had "Worms, Gravel or Plum stones or what."[3] She was haunted by the prospect of losing another child, especially now that happy, cheerful Francis had become such good company. He was sufficiently recovered to allow her to attend a ball on the 26th, but she was too fatigued to enjoy herself.

On 11 January, Elizabeth saw Colonel Beckwith, who brought her the first news that Simcoe had received a promotion. As of October, he was a major general in the army. As soon as he was informed, Simcoe wrote to Mary Anne Burges, asking her to place, with his tailor, an order for new regimentals. Once they were ready, she would arrange payment through Mr. Christopher Flood, the Simcoes' accountant, and find a means of sending them to Canada.[4] In one of her replies, Mary Anne let them know that a bust of General Wolfe, which Simcoe had ordered, had arrived at Wolford Lodge. It would remain in its box until he decided where he wanted it displayed. The bust of Lord Moira, she added, was sitting on top of a bookshelf, where it had become very dusty, although it could be cleaned. "I am impatient to become acquainted with Francis. You know I was the first person who predicted his future greatness; as that I expect to rise with him to fame".[5]

Replying to a letter of Elizabeth's of 2 January 1795, Mary Anne offered some advice:

> I think a little more stay at school may be just the thing for such an intractable temper as Sophia's. I wish she could be transported to Wolford Lodge, for a rebellious subject is really a great amusement to Mrs. Hunt; & she has had that relaxation for these two years past; Caroline being now quite as good as her Sisters ...[6]

By 31 January the governor had set out from York to meet them. Elizabeth had sent some of the baggage ahead to Montreal, where Captain Mayne would join them as their escort. She had admired Lord Dorchester's "Dormeuse", which she thought would be a suitable vehicle for the journey and she had ordered one made:

It is like an open Carriole with a head made of Seal Skin & lined with Baize, a large Bear or Buffalo skin fixes in front which perfectly secures you from wind & weather, & may be unhooked if the weather is fine or mild, a low seat & feather bed to keep one's feet warm.[7]

She gave up the house in Palace Street and took her entourage to Belmont. On 6 February, although Francis had a cold, they set out in the Dormeuse. At times Elizabeth found the cracking of the ice terrifying. After staying at some good, some less than clean houses, they reached Montreal, where Captain Mayne had already arrived. He followed the Dormeuse in a hired carriole loaded with baggage. They reached the home of James Gray, a half-pay major from Sir John Johnson's regiment, on the 11th. The governor was there; he had gone to Pointe au Baudet the day before, but they had not arrived, and he had returned to Major Gray's.

Elizabeth was delighted to see him, but the children gave him a boisterous welcome. On the 14th they arrived at Johnstown, where the governor had stayed earlier. In a house intended to be an inn, he had rented two large rooms, both well heated with stoves. There they found Major Littlehales, who had accompanied the governor. The journey, Elizabeth noted, "has quite established Francis's health though he was so ill when we left Quebec."[8] They planned to remain ten days at Johnstown, which was a mere townsite with a few houses on it. Elizabeth came down with a severe cold, leaving Collins the nurse in charge of the children. Whenever the governor and Major Littlehales had a moment, they took them out to wear off their energies.

On 23, 24 and 25 February very heavy snow fell, which made great sleighing fun for the children but dismayed their parents. Local men advised the governor that the road, a mere cart track, was impassable, but he would not listen. They left the heavy Dormeuse to be fetched later and proceeded in lighter carrioles. A party of volunteers ran in advance of the sleighs to pack down the tracks. The way led to the village of Lyn, and through the woods to Gananoque. They found the ice at the mouth of the Gananoque River very bad, and drove at breakneck speed "the safest way on rotten Ice."

Their next stop was Kingston, where they arrived on Sunday, 1 March. "We are comfortably lodged in the Barracks in Kingston. As there are few Officers here, we have the Mess room to dine in & a Room over it for the Gov.'s office, . ." These, as well as the kitchen, were detached from three more rooms they could use. "The drawing Room has not a stove in it which is a misfortune, but it is too late in the winter to be of much consequence & we have excellent wood fires."[9]

They were in Kingston much longer than expected. On 24 April Elizabeth wrote, "The Gov. has been so ill since the 21st March that I have not left his Room since that day." Collins was again in sole charge of the children, with Major Littlehales taking them out when his duties permitted. Simcoe had such a cough that he could not lie down. He tried to sleep in a chair, suffering from such headaches that he "could not bear any person but me to walk across the Room or speak loud." The only medical person Elizabeth could find was a horse doctor. Then Molly Brant came to the rescue.

When Molly heard of the governor's plight she sent Elizabeth a root (Elizabeth thought it was calamus) "which really relieved his Cough in a very short time."[10] The symptoms suggest bronchitis, or bronchial asthma, the same affliction that could have interfered during the visit of Prince Edward Duke of Kent to Newark. New paint in the barracks could have been a cause.

By then a letter was on the way from Mary Anne Burges with a consolatory comment on Sophia:

> I know not what to think of Sophia's temper; so unlike the rest of your children, ... I have no doubt but that future events of Sophia's life will be such as to require all that pertenacity of opinion, which you now may call stubbornness; but which will then acquire the name of very heroic firmness.[11]

By the beginning of May, Simcoe had recovered. Although Elizabeth had ague, they resolved to leave for York. They went aboard the *Onondaga* on 12 May. Contrary winds kept them in the harbour, which confirmed Simcoe's opinion of its drawbacks. On the 14th they watched the launching of a new schooner, the *Mohawk*. It came off the stocks with such force that for a moment they thought it would plough into the *Onondaga*. They sailed two p.m. on the 15th, after having to return to the harbour when a stiff gale arose. By five 5 p.m. on the 17th they were off Gibraltar Point. This time no pilot presented himself. When Simcoe discovered that the captain of the *Onondaga* was not sober, he decided to take a chance and "ordered the English lieutenant to give orders & he brought us safely into York Harbour." The night aboard had been very rough.

By that time an event of importance to all the Simcoes was the arrival at Tracey, Mary Anne Burges' home, of her first cousin, the Hon. Julia Somerville. Julia, who would celebrate her third birthday on 28 August 1795, had been orphaned, on 10 May, by the death of Mary Anne's uncle, Colonel Hugh Somerville. Julia was the youngest of nine children. The older ones were farmed out among other relatives. All of them agreed that Mary Anne would be a fitting guardian for Julia.

At first, Julia seemed the model child – until she overcame feelings of strangeness in her new home and began behaving normally:

> The trouble with my little girl has commenced...I am quite discouraged at the prospect I have with her ... I think myself the most unfortunate of any Monarch on earth, that Julia, my only subject, should prove a Jacobin.[12]

Mrs. Hunt offered to have Julia at Wolford Lodge, but she was planning to take the four Simcoe girls to the seaside at Seaton, "to bathe and strengthen them."[13] Mary Anne resolved to soldier on in the hope that so drastic a cure would not be necessary. Later she had to eat certain advice she had sent Elizabeth when she had complained about Sophia's temper. "Julia," Mary Anne admitted, "could match her."[14]

By 1 June, her ague improved and eager to see how the work had progressed, Elizabeth went by boat to Castle Frank. The children may have been with her, but she may also have found someone to give them lessons. On 6 June Francis celebrated his fourth birthday by giving a dinner to the soldiers' children. "The Shaws dined with him at an Upper Table." Rank counted. The Shaws were suitable playmates as the children of an officer.

As in 1794, the legislature would meet at Newark. Jay's Treaty would not come into effect for another year, and the troops still garrisoned Fort Niagara. Francis and Sophia, with servants and the baggage sailed on the *Onondaga* on 9 June. Elizabeth and the governor would go separately, along the shore in a large freight canoe, the gift of the Montreal-based Northwest Company. They were held up by rough weather until the 15th. They made the voyage in surprisingly good time, for they reached Navy Hall at eight o'clock on the 16th.

On 22 June, the family received some not very welcome guests, a party of French emigrants. They arrived at Fort Erie and came to Newark to ask Governor Simcoe's permission to travel to Lower Canada. Simcoe detained them, and sent a message to Lord Dorchester for instructions. While the Frenchmen were there, Elizabeth told her diary: "Their appearance is perfectly democratic & dirty."[15] "Democrat" was a dirty word to the Simcoes, one that Francis already knew meant dangerous radical. (Back home, little Julia Somerville was also catching on. When she was naughty she called herself a democrat.)[16]

A fortnight after Simcoe had asked for instructions Lord Dorchester replied. He did not want any French admitted to Lower Canada, where they might cause trouble among the French-speaking subjects. The Frenchmen returned to New York State on 22 July. The British garrison was still at Fort Niagara. Jay's Treaty, under which the British-occupied forts would be evacuated, had been passed on 24 June. However, it would not come into effect until after ratification. By the time the guns of Fort Niagara were in American hands, Simcoe knew that his government must be well beyond their range.

As the summer heat grew more intense, Elizabeth was longing for a way to escape from Navy Hall. She had made do long enough with the makeshift tents on the hillside and the oaken bower. On 11 August the Simcoes dined at the home of Christian, the widow of Gilbert Tice, who had been a captain in the Indian Department. The Tice house, on land above the walls of the gorge, would be the perfect place to be free of the humidity and fevers of Newark:

[We] arranged her consent to our staying a fortnight at her House. She is
to give us two Rooms & we are to have a Tent pitched for the Servants.
The situation is perfectly dry & healthy on the Mountain 5 miles from
the Fall of Niagara. There is a shed or gallery before the House & some
oak trees close to it, therefore there is always shade & cool air here,
when we are suffering from intense heat at Navy Hall.[17]

On the 15th the governor took the children by carriage to see the Falls and
Elizabeth rode part of the way. They took a tent and food and picnicked. Ten
days later Simcoe, Elizabeth and Francis drove to Fort Chippawa. The governor wanted to inspect the defences, but he became so ill that they returned temporarily to Newark. After a tent had been pitched, Francis noticed one of the
servants wading into Lake Ontario to wash some clothes:

Francis followed him up to his knees in water & sat on a Rock by him,
presently an Indian went to wash his cloaths & the group looked very
picturesque. Francis came back completely wet to fetch a loaf of bread to
give the Indian.

On Sunday, 30 July, Elizabeth decided to return to Mrs. Tice's, intending
to hold Francis before her saddle, but it was too hot to ride:

but having no Gentleman with me I was obliged to drive the Carriage
myself which I had never done & the roads are excessively rough till
after passing by the Falls. I tied Francis into the Carriage & drove him
very safely tho he complained of being much bruised & shook.[18]

The two weeks were only the beginning of the stay at Mrs. Tice's. In September, still there, Elizabeth put Francis in school. He was now four years and
four months old. Sophia was probably at the same school, but she was not
mentioned. "We walked Francis to the School where he goes every day a mile
from this house. He carries some bread & butter or Cheese for Dinner with
him & returns in the Evening."[19] She was now as glad to find a place where
Francis would have some discipline as she had been to find someone to take
over Sophia. Francis was still good natured, but he was big and active, with a
strength almost equal to her own. He had begun testing his mother, seeking to
establish the limits of her patience.

Letters which Elizabeth sent, to Wolford Lodge, to Mary Anne Burges
and to Mrs. Gwillim, were often recopied so that they could be handed round
other friends. To an unidentified recipient, Elizabeth had written:

Francis has come thru the heat better this summer and is stronger, we
have dipped him in the river for 10 minutes which I think has strength-

ened him. The Boy has a passion for ships, boats, cannons, paddling, roving etc., we may respect his will to become a sailor, you would laugh at his dancing & singing like the Indians, imitation so close it is ridiculous. The Gov. thought he might be frightened at war dances, instead he practises them.[20]

Francis, the report continued, attended all councils with the Indians, with great solemnity, dressed in a blanket, silver armbands above his elbows:

This will amuse Mrs. Graves. Mrs. Simcoe says it will soon be time to send him to school, because he has a great deal of sense and learns quickly, and being the only boy she has strong reason to suspect he's a bit spoiled at home.[21]

The last part of the letter is by Elizabeth herself.

"Francis is more afraid of his father than of me, who is sometimes obliged to call on the Gov." For John Graves Simcoe, Etonian and commissioned officer, corporal punishment was a natural phenomenon. A soldier in the ranks who broke a rule deserved to be tied to the halberts and flogged until his back resembled ground meat spread over exposed white bone. A sailor was strapped to a lattice for the cat-o-nine-tails. Schoolboy infractions earned the birch. The governor was far too wise to deprive his son of the benefits of a beating when required.

Now that late autumn had arrived, the time had come to return to York for the winter. On 2 October 1795, Elizabeth, children and servants left Mrs. Tice's for Navy Hall. Towards the end of the month, after a violent storm, they welcomed a few days of Indian summer. On 1 November the first snow fell. The 4th was fine and they breakfasted with Mrs. Hamilton.

At last, on 13 November they set sail for York. This time the vessel carrying the family, servants and baggage was a new small sloop, the *Governor Simcoe*.

Chapter 7
The Last Year in the Canadas

The *Governor Simcoe* arrived at York at five o'clock. Soon after they landed they drank tea with Mrs. John McGill. Elizabeth did not mention where they would be living. They were at the garrison, but whether they made do with the canvas houses again or had better accommodation she did not say. The first day of December was "A Summer day." By the 18th more seasonal temperatures prevailed.

> Francis brings all the Wood I burn in my Stove from the Wood Yard, I think the exercise is of service to him. He has today a little sledge to draw it upon.[1]

He was happy to find many friends. The Shaws were there, and John Simcoe Macaulay, a son of surgeon Dr. James Macaulay. John was not quite a year younger than Francis, who found him good company. During a visit to the Macaulay home, young John was cutting through large chunks of wood. Francis begged to be allowed to learn to handle an axe, too. Shivering at the sight of so sharp a blade, Elizabeth agreed to let him because he would be so useful.

York had grown, as everyone knew it would soon be the seat of government. Most of the civil servants and the officers of the Queen's Rangers now had 200-acre lots in the vicinity, and town lots as well. During a walk to the townsite on the 28th, the family watched a party depart to begin work on a road to what Elizabeth called the Pine Fort, which was on the Holland River that led to Lake Simcoe. The governor decided to name this important link to the upper lakes Yonge Street, after his friend, Sir George Yonge, Member of Parliament and then Secretary at War. Sir George was a neighbour back home. His country house, Escot [or Escott] was not far from Wolford Lodge and a place Francis would know well in later years.

On 6 January Elizabeth wrote to Mrs. Hunt. She wanted news of Charlotte, who had been ill when Mrs. Hunt had last written, She expressed her amazement at the the report of the progress the four girls at Wolford Lodge were making in their studies. Of Francis she wrote:

Francis will be a charming boy when he gets to Mr. Copplestone's where
we always intended to send him, but he wants a little of the discipline of
a school. His many illnesses, tender age and cleverness prevent me being
as strict with him as I should be & he is almost beyond my control.[2]

She was still worried at the prospect of war, but if they were at home General Simcoe would now be fighting in Flanders. The governor was now feeling healthy, which Elizabeth attributed to the cold season. On 7 January Mary Anne Burges wrote a very long letter. Much of it was her praise for Julia Somerville, who was adjusting well to life at Tracey. The temper displays were becoming rare when Julia found "how little she gains by them." Mary Anne promised to take heed of a caution the governor had written to her: for her [Julia's] sake & that of Francis as she had no way of knowing:

on which side the disastrous attachment may be formed because a lady
with such a name must build such a castle as in fairy tales & seclude her
from view of all the world & I must impersonate a dragon.[2]

What Mary Anne meant is hardly clear. Was Simcoe warning her against letting the child make unsuitable friendships or succumb to fortune hunters? The latter seemed hardly likely because Julia's inheritance would be modest. Or, was he match-making? From the point of view of parents and guardian, a union between Francis and Julia would give great satisfaction.

With the new year, the Simcoes were watching with keen interest the progress of the building of the summer home high above the Don River on Francis' land. Elizabeth enthused:

It is called Castle Frank built on the plan of a Grecian Temple, totally of
wood the logs squared & so grooved together that in case of decay any
log may be taken out. The large Pine trees make Pillars for the Porticos
which are at each end 16 feet high.[4]

Out of logs lying about they made a large fire near the house and dined on venison they toasted on forked sticks. They returned home in their carriole. Drives to Castle Frank were frequent. Venison was plentiful, usually shot by natives who sold it to the garrison. On 2 February they found that the carpenters had not yet installed a floor. Elizabeth was annoyed. Progress was slow because the workmen had taken time off to build a hut for themselves. Sometimes the governor accompanied them, when he could spare the time. He found the partly enclosed Dormeuse a boon during the cold weather, although the children liked to sit out in the front.

Elizabeth again mentioned Francis' small sleigh:

the servants have taught a goat to draw [the sleigh], he is the handsomest Goat I ever saw & looks very well in harness. It is a pretty sight to see Francis drawn in this Car. They used [taught] the animal to draw the sleigh by making him draw it full of wood, at first he was very untractable.[5]

Writing in March, Mary Anne Burges reported that the Reverend Mr. Copplestone was having trouble with some of his pupils. Two sons of a Mr. Quicke had been withdrawn from the school. The boys had lied about Copplestone and Mr. Quicke had persuaded Sir John de la Pole to withdraw his boy as well. This left Mr. Copplestone with only three scholars, and he wondered whether he would have to close the school. Next she reported that the three remaining boys had run away and got close to Exeter before Mr. Copplestone caught up with them. All three – two of them sons of the Simcoes' friend Edward Bastard – had returned home, which left the clergyman with no pupils. However, Mary Anne knew of two boys who would soon arrive. The good news was that Copplestone would have a space for Francis. Elizabeth could decide, when she got home, about the truth of certain tales circulating in Honiton.[6]

The winter dragged by. On 18 February the party who went to cut the road to Lake Simcoe returned after being away seven weeks. "The distance is 33 Miles & 56 Chains [a chain was 66 feet], they brought 2 Trout from Lake Simcoe weighing about 12 pounds each, but they are not as good as the smaller Trout." A friend, Mr. John Lawrence, who had accompanied the road workers, brought two small wooden bowls and spoons made by the natives... "The Children will use these bowls as basons [sic] at breakfast when travelling."[7]

Elizabeth rode to Castle Frank frequently, or took the children in a carriole when the snow conditions were right. March brought geese and blackbirds, signalling that spring could not be far off. She made no mention of a school, but as there were now quite a few children in the town they may have been meeting for lessons. By 18 April, Francis, who had been healthy through the coldest weather, was unwell:

We therefore set off to C. Frank today to change the air intending to pass some days there. The house being yet in an unfinished State, we divided the large Room by Sail Cloth, pitched the Tent on the inner part where we slept on wooden beds.

It is quite a Summer's day. Musquitos [sic] arrived at 3 o'clock. A large wooden canoe was launched here today built by one of the Men who ought to have been busy in working at Castle Frank.[8]

By the 20th, Francis was feeling much better, and was happily planting currant bushes and peach trees. They would not have much longer to enjoy

Castle Frank, because they expected to leave shortly for Niagara. Simcoe had decided to hold one more session of the legislature at Newark. It would be the last, however, because Jay's Treaty was to come into effect on 1 June and the garrison would soon have to evacuate Fort Niagara, leaving Newark unprotected. They sailed from York aboard the *Mohawk* on 29 April.

Ontario Archives

Castle Frank, the holiday home with Grecian columns that was built on Francis Simcoe's land above the Don River. Eventually it burned down.

The House of Assembly prorogued on 3 June, which Governor Simcoe then dissolved. The life of Newark as the capital ended on the 4th, with a ball in what Elizabeth called "a temporary room" attached to Navy Hall. By the 6th, Francis' fifth birthday, the family was packing up to return to York and the celebration was necessarily hasty. Attending was Lieutenant Robert Pilkington, of the Royal Engineers, a colleague who had accompanied the governor on many inspections. An excellent artist himself, Pilkington had drawn the boy's picture.

After bidding farewell to the Hamiltons, who had been so kind to them, on 7 June the Simcoes left Navy Hall for the last time, in the canoe, followed by a boat. For the parents, this was a journey of exploration of the land along the shore. For the most part the children and servants went by canoe or boat while the governor and Elizabeth rode horses. They rendezvoused to camp on land each night. Francis and Sophia went to the head of the lake, where their parents joined them and they finished the journey by water. They reached York on the 16th, nine days after leaving Newark.

By that time, the governor, who had been unwell for some weeks, had applied for a leave of absence. He needed to recover his health, but he also wanted to treat with the government directly. Lord Dorchester, who had consistently vetoed any plan for Upper Canada that involved much expenditure, had resigned. Simcoe hoped that by going to London, he might obtain permission directly for stronger defenses and to relocate the capital on the Thames River, without having to negotiate through another governor at Quebec.

On the 25th, Francis was again ill and feverish, and by the 29th Elizabeth was alarmed that he was no better and hoped that a change of air would cure him. The next day she sent the children by boat to Castle Frank, while she and the governor rode there through "these pleasant shady Pine Plains, now covered with sweet scented Fern." The plains were a fine place to ride because they were virgin forest, devoid of undergrowth. While their parents went back and forth, the children remained for most of the rest of their stay at Castle Frank, protected by nets from the ever annoying mosquitoes. Workmen had dug an underground room which was delightfully cool. On 18 July, Elizabeth reported, during a heavy rain shower "we were obliged to quit the lower Room the windows of which are not glazed – slept here." [9]

On the 14th, Simcoe learned that the government had granted his leave of absence. The frigate *Pearl*, Captain Samuel James Ballard, R.N., was at Quebec. He expected to sail on 10 August, which left little time for packing and farewells. On 20 July the children left Castle Frank for the last time. They had found it a delightful place. They ran along shaded footpaths or looked for toads and other pets more exotic than Jack Sharp or the cat. Often they were joined by friends who came to visit. When they returned to the garrison they found their mother in tears and inconsolable at the thought of leaving her dear friends.

Sophia had a tendency to imitate Elizabeth, but Francis, more inclined to wait and see, wondered whether he, too, should feel sad. He was at best puzzled. He was leaving the only way of life he had known for a place of mystery called Wolford Lodge and a school which Papa, when displeased, made sound like a threat.

On the 21st, while their mother "cried all day", the Gov. dined with Captain John McGill. At three o'clock they went aboard the *Onondaga* while the other vessels in the harbour fired a salute. Winds were light, and they did not reach Kingston until late on the night of the 25th. They left the next morning in bateaux. They were carrying home some unusual items – the canoe and a sleigh, beaver blankets and other souvenirs for themselves and relatives and friends. By that time travel in the near-wilderness had become routine. Francis noticed that Mama seemed strangely alarmed as they rushed down the Long

Sault Rapids. Elizabeth admitted that she had been less terrified during their last trip because she was too worried about Simcoe's safety in the event of war to think about the rapids.[10]

They reached Montreal on 30 July, and stayed at the home of Mr. William Henry Gray, postmaster and a friend from previous visits. The 31st was a Sunday. The commander of the Montreal garrison, General Gariel Christie, loaned them his coach for the ride to church.

"Why, it's a room on wheels!" Francis exclaimed.

He could remember riding only in open carriages, other than the Dormeuse. When they visited the country house of the fur trader, Joseph Frobisher, two dog houses at the front door caught Francis' attention. He was used to seeing sentries on duty wherever the governor stayed.

"Do people here keep dogs as Centinels?" he enquired.[11]

On 5 August they reached Belmont House, to a warm welcome from Colonel and Mrs. Caldwell. In the morning they received a message from the Anglican Bishop Jacob Mountain, whose child died during the night, offering the Simcoes the use of his house in Quebec. With his family, he would be going to Trois Rivières, to the home of his brother, Reverend Jehosophat Mountain, for a period of mourning.

Although saddened they were grateful. Mrs. Robert Prescott, the wife of the incoming governor in chief, had complained about their miserable lodgings before the Dorchesters had vacated the château. The outgoing Dorchesters left Quebec on 9 August aboard the *Active*. Meanwhile the *Pearl*, on which the Simcoes expected to sail, had gone on a cruise but was supposed to return by the 10th. By the 16th the Pearl was still away. News arrived that the *Active* had been wrecked off the Isle of Anticosti, but everyone was safe and the Dorchesters had been taken to Gaspé. They expected the *Pearl* to take them to Halifax. On the 18th Elizabeth wrote: "We are under great enxiety least Lord Dorchester should take the *Pearl* to carry him to England from Hallifax [sic]."

Her worry proved groundless; the *Pearl* returned from Halifax on 3 September. Captain Ballard informed the Simcoes that he would sail on the 10th, just a month later than originally planned. The delay brought John Graves Simcoe the opportunity to demonstrate his organizational skills. As they were getting into a carriage to accept an invitation from the Prescotts to the château, they found that the street was full of smoke – a terrifying prospect in a city with many wooden buildings and roofed invariably with wood shingles. Word reached the men at the Prescotts' that the fire had begun in a barn and was raging in St. Louis Street and approaching Bishop Mountain's house.

Gen'l Simcoe immediately went there & remained the whole afternoon giving directions to some of the Crew of the Pearl by whose exertions the Bishop's House & Houses adjoining were saved tho' they several times caught fire. Mrs. Prescott & I were looking out from the Upper windows when we saw a spark on the Recollect Church & in a few minutes thw whole building was in a blaze.[12]

Fortunately the Simcoes had been about to leave the bishop's house to spend the last few days with Chief Justice William Osgoode (who had been the first chief justice of Upper Canada before his promotion to Quebec). Their baggage and the children and servants were already there. When Elizabeth went to Mr. Osgoode's to change her clothes, she found the children so excited and eager to see what was happening that she took them into Palace Street. There they stayed until eight o'clock when "Gen'l Simcoe came to fetch us to the Chief Justice's."

They embarked on the *Pearl* on 10 September, a Saturday, as planned. Elizabeth's cabin as larger than on the *Triton*, but "the Guns are very commodious." In the event of an attack by French ships, she was expected to clear the cabin of all baggage so that the guns could be put in position.

The voyage was nerve wracking. The *Pearl* was convoying several merchant ships that could not keep up. They ran aground once, and the *Pearl* was sailing badly in order to keep back with the merchantmen. The only one who was completely happy was Francis, who adored being at sea and was never sick. Captain Ballard had two dogs, Beau and Belle, "who are his constant play fellows. He is determined to be a sailor."

During one horrendous gale, "We ran 9 knots an hour under bare poles." (This was a rare speed for a vessel with all sails furled.) By 11 October they were close to Berry Head and intending to be put ashore at Tor Bay, conveniently close to Wolford Lodge. The wind did not cooperate. They were blown along the south coast and passed Dover on the 12th. By the 13th they were "in the Downs." and they landed at Deal the following day and took rooms at an inn. Sophia, who had wearied of the seven-week voyage, was relieved to be on firm ground. Elizabeth parted with the various officers with regret. Captain Leveson Gower, commander of the lost ship *Active*, had returned with them. Both he and Captain Ballard offered to do whatever they could should Francis resolve on the Royal Navy:

From my experience of people I am as anxious he should be a sailor as he is to be one. Francis came down stairs at the Inn backwards, as he used to descend the Ladder on board the Pearl. I found it a great happiness to find the Rooms steady & not roll like the Ship.[13]

The journey was far from over. They set out for Canterbury in a hired coach, and on to London; the heavy baggage and most of the servants would follow in wagons. The grey sky depressed Elizabeth. Everything seemed so damp and cheerless "from the want of our bright Canadian Sun that the effect was striking & the contrast very unfavourable to the English climate."

They reached an inn in Cork Street, London, on the 16th. where they stayed a few days. General Simcoe wanted to spend some time with the commander in chief's staff at Horse Guards, justifying the plans he had made for Upper Canada and seeking to promote them for the good of the province. Simcoe had decisions to make. Should he return to Upper Canada once his health had improved, or would the officers suggest other duties for him? Rumours circulated that he might be the successor to Robert Prescott as governor in chief of both the Canadas.

Meanwhile, Francis and Sophia waited, trying to imagine what Wolford Lodge would look like. What were their older sisters like, and Miss Burges and Julia? And where were the glorious red leaves of the maples and oaks? Why did the sky continually drop drizzle that went on and on? In Upper Canada, when it rained it usually rained hard and got it over with.

Part Two
School Days 1796-1807

Chapter 8

Mr. Copplestone's Pupil and King's School

E arly in November the Simcoe entourage arrived at Honiton and left the highroad for the narrower carriage road that led towards Hembury Fort House then branched northeast to Wolford. Francis stared, taking in the utterly new look of the pretty Devonshire landscape. Neat hedgerows blocked the view of many of the largest houses. Gateways with gate houses allowed glimpses of massive buildings, of parkland – trees planted in rows along drives, vast spreading lawns where horses, cattle and sheep grazed. They passed through a tiny village of thatched cottages where agricultural labourers and craftsmen lived, with its substantial stone parish church.

At last they entered the wide, neat laneway beyond their own gatehouse, and there it stood, just as massive as the others, of grey stone. He counted seven windows along the second floor of the facade, and nine along the west side. Wolford Lodge dwarfed Belmont, the Caldwell house, and even the Château St. Louis seemed smaller. Behind, other buildings were hidden by a small forest. That, at least, felt familiar, although the trees were not very tall and the ground below them had manicured paths. The scene was so different from the wild trails through the Upper Canadian woods. Francis could not imagine Yonge Street ever becoming so tamed.

Papa, with his military sense of timing, must have let Mrs. Hunt know exactly when to expect them, for there, standing in the driveway in front of the wide doorway was a crowd of people. Mama left the carriage first, followed at once by Sophia, who jumped down eagerly. Francis waited until Papa had alighted before attempting to exit. What a confusing few minutes followed. Mama introduced Mrs. Hunt first, then Miss Hunt. Twelve-year-old Eliza came forward shyly and curtseyed to her parents, followed by Charlotte and Harriet, who were taller, and Caroline, smaller than Sophia and himself. Mama seemed shy, but Papa gathered the four eldest girls to himself, hugging then, eyes damp, calling to Sophia and Francis to come, too. Papa had broken the ice, and soon Mama was hugging the sisters of whom Francis had no recollection and was still trying to sort out which was which.

That was not all. He could hardly believe how many servants were lined up, waiting to greet Mama and Papa. And where could the remarkable Miss Burges be in all this hubbub? Eliza answered the question. She left the group and returned accompanied by a small, dark, plump woman who held the hand of a little girl. He did not have to be told that here was his mother's closest friend, and her ward, the four-year-old Hon. Julia Somerville.

Simcoe had Francis follow him, as the son and heir, while he greeted the house and estate servants. The men bowed, and the women dropped their curtseys, then they left for their duties and the family went inside to a vast hallway and on to what Mama called the morning room, where tea had been laid out on several tables. Talk was rather difficult for people who had yet to be truly acquainted. The four strange sisters were appallingly well behaved, and made their replies scarcely above a whisper. Even Sophia was overawed by such formality, but Mama seemed delighted with them.

Francis quickly discovered that Miss Burges was everything he had hoped. She had an easy manner that encouraged him to talk freely, and from the beginning they were good companions. With Mama busy setting her home to rights after five years, and Papa in his study writing reports for the government, Francis explored the grounds with Miss Burges. Sometimes he walked to Tracey, a somewhat smaller house than Wolford Lodge, set in pretty grounds. He romped with the dog, Ranger, of whom Miss Burges had written to Mama, and had rides on her small horse, Placid, hoping that soon Papa would let him have a pony of his own.

A few days later the heavy baggage arrived from Deal, and Papa delighted in handing out presents, and showing the older girls the canoe and sleigh they had brought as souvenirs, the beaver and bear skins, and the stove that they would install in the Wolford Lodge kitchen as soon as pipes could be made in Honiton. Afterwards Mrs. Hunt and Miss Hunt left Wolford Lodge, their work as housekeeper and tutor at an end, and moved to Bath. Later, Great Aunt Margaret Graves informed Eliza, with whom she kept up a frequent correspondence, that Miss Mary Hunt was in the household of four-year-old Princess Charlotte of Wales, the only child of the (feuding) Prince and Princess of Wales. A great honour for the Hunts, Mrs. Graves added.[1]

Francis thoroughly explored Wolford Lodge, getting to know what was where. The children's quarters were a large nursery on the second floor, but the rest of the house was a challenge. It lent itself so well to games of hide and seek, and it had so many places where a small boy who did not want to be found could conceal himself so that he would not be given some dreary task.

Two weeks had sped by, and the time had come for Francis to enter Mr. Copplestone's school, four miles off in Honiton. Mama attended to packing the right clothes. The rifle shirts and trousers remained behind. With him would go new shirts with ruffled cuffs, breeches with matching waistcoat and coat, new woolen stockings and shoes with buckles from the local shoemaker, a tricorne hat and new greatcoat. A Quebec-made cream-coloured blanket coat with wide red stripes, tuque and sash, had been fine for the Canadas, but not for civilization.

Papa took time off from his work to accompany Francis in the carriage, which was cold comfort. Papa assured him how much he would love school, but Francis remembered that Papa expected the clergyman to reform him and he adopted a wait-and-see stance. Mr. Copplestone's was typical of many small schools kept by clergymen who took pupils to supplement their incomes from the parish. A few boys boarded with the rector. Fortunately rectories were intended for large families and Mr. Copplestone had plenty of room for half a dozen boys. He had a large room that served as a dormitory, and a schoolroom with chairs and tables where he gave the boys their lessons. Mrs. Copplestone, the rector's wife, was in charge of their meals and enforced a measure of cleanliness, assisted by housemaids and a cook. Boys from other such small schools joined with Mr. Copplestone's for games and formed teams. Francis particularly enjoyed cricket, which he played well.

On 19 November, Elizabeth's aunt, Mrs. Gwillim, wrote from Old Court, the Gwillim estate at Whitchurch, in Herefordshire. She was happy to hear that her niece had found everyone well at Wolford Lodge. "You show fortitude leaving your Little Man". Boys, she continued, were better educated under men, and the Simcoes' choice of a clergyman was wise. Religion and the right morals were a safeguard against temptation.[2]

Francis appeared to settle down without difficulty. He had to adjust to this strange new setting, of substantial houses, but ones that were usually much colder than the houses, tents and forts where he had lived most of his life. He found no stoves in the Copplestone rectory. Warm clothes, so unsuitable in the Canadian summer, were now necessary most of the year. Despite his exotic upbringing thus far, Francis was cautious. He seemed to grasp instinctively that his schoolfellows were not in the least interested in hearing about Canada, or about Indian councils, or native dances. He kept his memories to himself, relieved that Mama had not allowed him to bring his rifle shirt or his Indian blanket. He recalled that even boys at York and Niagara, who were inclined to defer to the governor's son, had made him aware that boys who were different were likely to be teased, or bullied.

By December the War Office had a new task for Major General Simcoe. He was to go to San Domingo as governor and commander-in-chief. When Francis set out for his Christmas holiday, he was looking forward to the kind of festivities of earlier years that his parents had described. He found the family in a subdued mood. Mama was unhappy because Papa had accepted the appointment to hot, steamy San Domingo. Some ghastly fever would be certain to damage his health. Papa, busy getting ready to sail, had not had time to write a Christmas play and the number of invited guests was small.

They included, however, a very special houseguest, Mr. William Walcot, from Oundle, Northamptonshire, of whom Francis had heard much. Elizabeth's parents were Mr. Walcot's second cousins, making her his second cousin once removed. He was a wealthy bachelor with large estates and a fine town house in Oundle.[3]

Mr. Walcot was a close friend of General Simcoe's, who helped care for properties Elizabeth had inherited from her mother's family. Walcot and Simcoe were conducting a friendly rivalry over the merits of their alma maters; Walcot was a Cambridge man, Simcoe an Oxonian. When the time came, Mr. Walcot insisted, Francis would be much happier at Cambridge. Of course, Papa disagreed. Francis, yet to be introduced to Latin or Greek, felt confused.

Francis had returned to Mr. Copplestone's before Papa's departure for San Domingo. In the end Simcoe did not leave until spring. Afterwards Mama took Francis' five sisters to visit their great aunt, Margaret Graves, at Bath. Leaving them there, Elizabeth went to London and did not return until July. She stopped in Honiton and took Francis home for the summer holiday. He had celebrated his sixth birthday at school. Lessons so far consisted of penmanship and drawing, reading, arithmatic, French and memorizing Church of England catechism. In a year or two, however, he would move on to King's School in Ottery St. Mary, where the emphasis would be on the classics, and the boys would spend most of their time studying Latin and Greek. Mama was delighted to hear from Mr. Copplestone that Francis showed a true aptitude for drawing. Already she had begun taking his sisters on sketching expeditions, and she looked forward having him join them.

By August Papa was on his way home from San Domingo. In October, when Francis was back at school, Simcoe returned to Wolford Lodge in an angry mood. As in Upper Canada, the government had not given him enough troops and other support to do the work demanded of him. Not long afterwards the government decided that sending any more troops in an attempt to rule San Domingo was a waste and ordered the island evacuated. Because Simcoe was the last British governor of San Domingo, King George III gave him "two Brass Spanish guns".[4] These weapons later graced the front hall of Wolford lodge

By 1798 Francis, now nearly eight, heard talk of returning to Quebec. Papa might be the next governor in chief after Robert Prescott. Mama was delighted at the prospect, and Francis was hoping he might resume the old life, with its bright, sunny winters. They would not go until the spring of 1799, because he was to have a new brother or sister in July 1798. Mrs. Gwillim wrote that she hoped the baby would be another boy. The Irish situation, she contended, looked ominous. Many people disapproved of Prime Minister Pitt's solution of union with Britain and Catholic emancipation. The Catholic Duke of Norfolk's influence was already making the country disloyal.[5] The plan for Canada was shelved when Ireland was torn by rebellion. Major-General Simcoe received command of all the troops in the southwest of England.

John Cornwall Simcoe was born on 7 July 1798. Great Aunt Margaret Graves wrote Eliza that she thought boys a "domineering set of beings" but, as Eliza had written her, they had "girls enow." [6] Francis' feelings were mixed. Of course, everyone told him how lucky he was to have a brother, but he might also be losing his special status. He would no longer be cock of the walk.

As the other children had been, Baby John was inoculated with smallpox material. On 13 October Mrs. Gwillim wrote that she hoped "our little Man" was safe from all danger of the smallpox for his life:

> but as Chicken pox is about who ever inoculated him ought to be particu-
> larly careful of mistakes ... but by your mentioning the ninth day it looks
> as to be the right sort the other drys [sic] away sooner.[7]

She was wrong; John contracted the serious form. Severely weakened, he was never strong afterwards, and he died on 22 March 1799 at Wolford Lodge. Francis mourned. For a while he had to find a place by himself where he could have a good, unmanly cry. John had become a real person and his heart had warmed to the tiny boy. At the time of John's death Francis was home from school. Both he and Caroline were very ill with whooping cough, which added to their mother's worry and sorrow. Elizabeth had lost two children in a row – little Katherine who lay at York, and now John. On the grounds of the Wolford estate were ruins that had been built by members of Cistercian Order. Here some of the monks had been buried. The grieving father decided he would build the Simcoe family chapel on the grounds of these ruins, and he laid out a burial plot. John Cornwall Simcoe was the first of the family to be interred there.

When Caroline and Francis had recovered fully, Papa rented a house in Plymouth, as his headquarters, and Mama, who felt the need for a change of scene, went to be with him for an indefinite stay. There, on 28 February 1800, Mama gave birth to her ninth child, another son. They named him Henry Addington Simcoe, in honour of Papa's colleague and a future prime minister. Henry thrived, a boy Francis came to adore.

On 30 April, from Plymouth, General Simcoe wrote a rather odd letter to nine-year-old Francis, starting with "My dear son":

> the expedition on which I was going has been laid aside, to my great
> Mortificaiton as an English gentleman & an English statesman, but to my
> great satisfaction as the Father of Francis Simcoe, whom I shall hope to
> find a very good boy on my return to my command in Devonshire, which
> will be shortly. Your Affectionate Father, J.G. Simcoe [8]

The relationship that seemed so spontaneous earlier now seemed quite formal. Nowhere in his own letters did Francis refer to his father, except with a politeness that lacked warmth. In the earliest letter still in existence, dated 28 June 1806, when John Graves Simcoe was still alive, Francis did not mention him. Simcoe habitually lectured his children, and Francis likely more than his sisters. In the above letter "very good boy" seems almost a threat. Simcoe did not say what expedition had been "laid aside", but it was important and a more worthy command than that of the West Country. If his relationship with his first son was growing cool, Simcoe had a much warmer one with Eliza, his eldest daughter, whose letters do show him affection. Did his expectations weigh heavily on the shoulders of the young boy?

On 6 August, Elizabeth received word that Mrs. Gwillim, her common sense aunt, had died at Whitchurch. Mrs. Graves wrote a sympathy letter to Eliza. The occasion was sad, but Mrs. Gwillim had endured such suffering that the end was a release.[9] Francis had not known this great aunt well because he had visited Old Court only briefly during school holidays.

As the year ended and 1801 began, the holiday festivities at Wolford Lodge were as the Simcoe parents had described them during the quieter celebrations at Newark and York. For New Year Papa had planned a great masquerade of Shakespeare's characters which Caroline Simcoe described in a letter to Mrs. Hunt, who was still living in Bath. Elizabeth was an onlooker who took no part. She was expecting her tenth child in March.

Father, Caroline wrote, as Prospero from The Tempest, introduced everyone. Miss Burges was "the drollest figure in the room" as a witch from Macbeth. Julia Somerville was Moth, with enormous wings. Eliza was Thisbe; Charlotte, Pyramus; Harriet, Wall; Sophia, Moonshine; and Francis, Lion. Later they all changed costumes. Francis was Oberon, King of the Fairies; Caroline was Titania the Queen; Sophia was Ariel; Julia represented Nimrod's ghost. A band from Honiton played for dancing and a "pedlar" distributed presents. "Henry," she finished, "is very well & I hope will soon be able to walk alone."[10]

As of 1 January 1801, Simcoe was promoted a lieutenant general in the army, which may have soothed his wounded pride over the cancelling of the expedition the previous year. Elizabeth's tenth child, born on 23 March 1801, was a daughter they named Katherine. Like her predecessor who died at York early in her second year, the baby was named for Simcoe's mother, Katherine Stamford. Early in the summer, Mrs. Graves accepted a long-standing invitation to visit Wolford Lodge. She had not been back since she had purchased the house in Bath and moved there. Although she had turned down invitations from her niece, the general was able to charm her into coming. Eliza was comfortable with the old lady, but Francis, and most of the younger ones, preferred to stay out of her way. Miss Burges, who was quick to notice, happily admitted that in her youth she found Great Aunt Margaret a holy terror.

Meanwhile, the workmen had been erecting Wolford Chapel next to the plot where John Cornwall Simcoe lay. On 19 August, a Thursday, Simcoe wrote to the Reverend John Pratt, the rector of the parish church at Dunkeswell, asking him to attend the dedication of the chapel, "on Monday next" (23 August) at Eleven o'clock:

> before our most valued Relation Mrs. Graves returns to Bath. I shall be obliged to you for a Sermon on the occasion & I should wish the text to be "as for me and my House, we will serve the Lord," an inscription that hereafter will be placed in the Church – [Chapel].[11]

Since August was holiday time, Francis was at home and did not need to be summoned from King's School. Wolford Lodge lay in the parish of Dunkeswell. The parish church, which the Simcoes attended regularly, had been built next to ancient Dunkesell Abbey, of stones from the abbey ruins. Here Francis would have seen poverty, some of it caused by enclosure of the common lands that had left people without grazing for their livestock. Some of the poor had built hovels from abbey stones; others had burrowed into the ruins for shelter. Most lingered along the roads and parks, hoping for hand-outs. Simcoe himself had purchased common lands and improved them, which he considered necessary. The old open field and common grazing system had become very inefficient and productivity was too low. He convinced his family that the real answer to poverty was homes in Upper Canada or work in the growing towns. Serving the Lord meant helping the poor to help themselves, which he did by employing many labourers on his estates and supporting common schools for the catechizing of the children of the poor.

The holiday celebrations at Wolford Lodge in January 1802 were even more spectacular than the year before. Eliza, now eighteen, described them in a letter to Miss Hunt. "Father" had written a play based on Joseph Addison's Roman tragedy Cato. "Mother" had dressed the cast. Francis was Decius and his school fellows acted other parts. Caroline spoke the prologue and Julia the epilogue, and Sophia was a senator. Again the house was full of company, and everyone danced until two a.m.

Julia, dressed as Britannia, began:

> Ye British youth, be worth like thus approved, And shew that you have Virtue to be moved From Greece, from Rome, your first Examples draw, And learn to reverence your Countries' law ...

It ended:

> Kindle in all, a never dying flame And prove you worthy of your Countries fame.[12]

The last Simcoe child, named Anne, arrived on 31 July 1804. Francis left King's School for the last time only days before.[13] In September he would go to Eton, following in his father's footsteps. About that time the Simcoes decided to have a second home on the Devonshire coast, where they could stay during school holidays, or when the sea air would restore anyone to good health. They chose a villa overlooking the sea at Budleigh Salterton, a little fishing port at the mouth of the Otter River. Francis spent many happy hours gathering clams when the tide was out, or exploring the neighbourhood with his sisters and Julia.

Chapter 9
Eton College 1804-1807

In 1804 Eton was England's most fashionable public (private) school, and so it remains. Founded in 1440 by King Henry VI, King's College of our Lady, the original name, was (like many of the first grammar schools in England) intended for the education of poor boys. Known as King's scholars, the number to be educated in the classics was set at seventy. These free scholars lived in a huge dormitory and took their meals within the school building. Boys from families who could afford to pay for their education were not excluded, but they could not live in the college. Such resided in boarding houses in the town, and were therefore called Oppidans. Many of the boarding houses were owned and operated, for profit, by masters and assistant masters of the College. When Francis Simcoe entered Eton, it accommodated about 500 boys. The number of King's Scholars remained at seventy. They still lived in, while all the others were Oppidans. (When Eton celebrated its 450th anniversary in 1990, the enrolment had reached 1,275 boys; the number of scholars remained at seventy.)[1]

Francis took to Eton like the proverbial duck to water. He was the happiest he had ever been, with the possible exception of his carefree days in Upper Canada. The boys rose very early, worked long hours in the schoolrooms, and had long study periods as well. Bedtime was also early. Yet there were compensations. On certain days they were allowed free time to pursue special interests, and plenty of time for games. He especially loved cricket. The Duke of Wellington never actually said the Battle of Waterloo was won on the playing fields of Eton, but the myth that the boys did not play cricket is equally incorrect. Francis wrote that they did.[2] New boys had to fag for their elders, but Francis did not find this burdonsome. His natural good nature eased him through humiliation and an athletic quickness helped him obey demands with alacrity.

The headmaster when Francis arrived was the popular Rev. Dr. Joseph Goodall, under whom the school was flourishing. He understood boys, and had scant difficulty controlling high spirits or outright unacceptable behaviour. He rarely resorted to use of the school's infamous birching block. His floggings were less severe than during the reigns of the headmasters who preceded and followed him. (In 1808, after he had received his first commission, Francis wrote from London that he had paid a visit to Eton, and he longed to return to those carefree days.)[3]

John Graves Simcoe had not been as fortunate. His headmaster, Dr. John Foster, was a brilliant classical scholar, but he had trouble keeping order. That he was the son of a tradesman in Windsor did not help. Many of the "young gentlemen" viewed him with scorn. Matters came to a head in the autumn of 1768, when masters attempted to curtail the right of senior boys to be in the town of Eton. The boys objected on the grounds that as long as they were not found in taverns, billiard rooms or other forbidden premises they were within their rights. When Dr. Foster stood firm, the praepostors (prefects), most sixth form boys, and some from the fifth and fourth forms, left the school.[4]

A poem written by one of Simcoe's friends, William Boscawen, suggests that the sixteen-year-old future general was among the rebels. Standing up for what he believed were his rights was in character:

With you [Simcoe] rebellions chance I tried
Old Foster's threats, his arm defied
And dar'd his empire mock
But oh, how short our glory's fate
How few escaped The Block.[5]

Many of the boys made their way home and were allowed to leave Eton, but most were sent back to be punished savagely by Dr. Foster. Simcoe had no alternative but to return to the school, line up with others to await his turn to kneel and bend over the birching block. As the son of a widowed mother with limited assets he could not afford to be expelled. He had resolved on the army. His mother had the means to purchase subalterns' commissions, but not enough influence to have disgraceful conduct overlooked.

The practice of purchase of commissions was corrupt. In 1770, when Simcoe was commissioned ensign, sixteen was supposed to be the minimum age for this commission. Wealthy, titled fathers could buy one sooner, by offering more than the legal rate of £400. Records show purchases for boys as young as seven years old. The boy would take up the commission later, but he would be allowed seniority from the date of purchase. Promotion depended on seniority, not competence. Thus a boy whose commission had been purchased at age seven might jump the queue and claim nine years of seniority when he actually joined his regiment.

By the time Francis entered Eton, he was contemplating his ultimate future. As a five-year-old he decided on the navy, but now he looked at other alternatives. Mr. William Walcot, still recommending Cambridge, wanted him to study law. Father, continuing his verbal sparring with Mr. Walcot, voted for

Merton College at Oxford. Francis quickly noted that Eton boys referred to their sires as Father or the Pater or "the Guv". Papa was for children.

He could imitate his father, by having a year or so at Oxford before deciding on the law, the navy, or the army. By June 1806, when he turned fifteen, he had resolved on the army, and as soon as possible. He was willing to go into a line infantry regiment which was less costly than the cavalry units.[6] He did not want to attend Oxford first, nor study law at Cambridge, even for a year. He wanted his ensign's commission at age sixteen, and he intended to take his profession very seriously and to become every bit as fine an officer as his father, or better. Recently the army had been reformed by Prince Frederick Augustus Duke of York. As commander in chief, he had forbidden early purchase of commissions. An ensign had to be sixteen, although he might purchase a lieutenancy in a matter of months if a vacancy occurred. He then had to serve four years before he could qualify to purchase a captaincy. He might have to serve longer than four years as a subaltern, because he would only be permitted to purchase when all the lieutenants in the army who were senior to him had purchased their promotions.

Francis had already demonstrated competence. At Eton he had begun to draw accurate maps, line drawings and sketches of buildings and towns, using pens with tiny steel nibs that allowed him to do very fine handwork. Most of the best visual records left for posterity wherever the British army was stationed were drawn by officers trained to make precise representations. On 28 June he wrote to "My dear Mother" from Eton. "Mama" was as juvenile as "Papa". This was the earliest letter Francis wrote that is extant. It was well expressed. Puzzling is the strange absence of any message for his father. The Mr. Cholwich he referred to was a family friend from Devon who visited him at Eton:

> I have decided to go into the army & told Mr. Cholwich & have no objection to go into the Line, especially as Lord Moira has been so good as to offer me his assistance. Mr. Walcot at one time wished me to study the Law, and I had some thoughts of it then as he seemed to wish it very much, but now I am determined to go into the Army.[7]

The former Francis Lord Rawdon, Francis' father's colleague during the American Revolution, had inherited the title 2nd Earl of Moira from his father, the 1st Earl. Lord Moira was the Honorary Colonel of the 27th Inniskilling Regiment of Foot and still a man with enormous respect and devotion to General Simcoe. The regimental depot was at Enniskillen, in County Fermanagh, a strongly Protestant area (one of the six counties of Northern Ireland after partition). Prior to Catholic Emancipation in 1829, officially, commissioned officers had to be Protestants, although a favoured few were not. Non-commissioned officers and the rank and file could be Roman Catholics. The rank and file of the 27th Foot were also mainly Protestants but some had been recruited in Roman Catholic areas.

Simcoe was pleased with Moira's offer to support an application for a commission. He was also happy to have Francis serving with an infantry regiment, the backbone of the army. The general's first commission had been in the 35th Foot.The cavalry might be the more dashing, but infantry was versatile; infantry won wars.

At the time of Francis' first letter, Lieutenant General Simcoe was about to be appointed governor general of India, and with the promise of a peerage. He owed this success mainly to the influence of Henry Addington, prime minister from 1801 until 1804 and in 1806 a member of Prime Minister Lord Grenville's "Ministry of all the Talents". Elizabeth was delighted and looking forward to going with Simcoe, and taking most of the girls and Henry. Accommodation for the viceregal family would not be the problem they had faced in Upper Canada. Francis would remain at Eton until he was sixteen and could be commissioned. He was disappointed to miss the opportunity, but he had his own agenda over which he did not want to waste any time.

Before Simcoe could set out for India, the government had another assignment for him. He was to join a team of officers being sent to Portugal to assess the situation there, and to recommend whether or not Britain should send troops to support the Portuguese against threats from Spain. The fact-finding group set sail in the *Illustrious*, which was newly commissioned, and which entered the mouth of the Tagus River in late August. By that time Simcoe was dangerously ill, the most likely cause the exceedingly toxic fumes from the new paint. The physicians consulted recommended pure air, and the general was taken by coach to the university town of Coimbra, in high country north of Lisbon. From there he wrote to Eliza on 13 September 1806. He had been extremely ill but had recovered apace. He had been removed to this "charming romantic spot for pure air and begin to feel its benefits ... assure all under my own hand of my abounding love and affection. J.G. Simcoe" [8]

Soon after he wrote, he was taken back to stay on the ship and he was soon too ill to continue. The *Illustrious* sailed for Tor Bay, Devonshire and put him aboard a small boat on 20 October. A coach took him to Exeter and left him at the home of Archdeacon George Moore, near the cathedral. Word was sent express to Elizabeth, then in London with some of her daughters, shopping in preparation for going to India. A message went to Eton to tell Francis to come as quickly as possible.

With his wife and some of his children by his side General Simcoe breathed his last on 26 October. He had not been able to recover from the effects of the poisonous paint fumes he had had to breathe on the return voyage.[9] For Francis, the loss of his father was a tragedy, but in a way it was also a release. For his mother, the funeral arrangements were her immediate concern. As Simcoe had intended, they would require as much attention as a military operation.

The family remained in Exeter from Sunday 26 October until Tuesday 4 November, the day of the funeral. A commemoration worthy of this important military man took time to organize. Many friends and colleagues had to be notified. Charlotte Simcoe, writing to Miss Hunt, maintained that Miss Mary Anne Burges had injured her already indifferent health by coming to Elizabeth's side. An account of the funeral appeared in the Exeter *Flying Post* on Thursday 6 November:

> On Tuesday the remains of the late much lamented General Simcoe were removed from his apartments at the rev. Archdeacon Moore's, in this city, to his family seat at Wolford Lodge, for interment. The funeral was most respectably attended; three mourning coaches followed the hearse, in which were the chief mourners, the confidental friends of the late general, and his servants. After them came the general's carriage, attended by two servants in deep mourning on horsback... All the troops having quitted this city on account of the election, the Exeter regiment of volunteers assembled at the three-mile stone on the Honiton road, to pay a compliment to the deceased general. From thence his remains were escorted by a squadron of dragoons, the volunteers assembling at various passes to line the road, whilst the procession passed on. At Honiton the troops were all drawn out, and minute guns fired. In short, every respect which could be paid to an esteemed and much-lamented commander was shown on this occasion. The body was interred by torchlight, about six in the evening.[10]

According to John Bailey, a servant of the Simcoes, when the Luppitt Company of Artillery (volunteers who had been raised by the general) fired as the body was being put into the grave, the noise shook the entire house. Great Aunt Margaret Graves, too elderly to attend the ceremony, advised Eliza that time was the best healer. Best wishes to "Mother and her dear children" especially six-year-old Henry, who was too young to understand what he had lost.[11]

The loss left Francis with an emptiness, but his main concern was for his mother, who did not have time to mourn. She had to become head of the family immediately, and she insisted that he return to Eton as soon as possible so that he would be ready for his commission next year. Under no circumstances would she allow him to change any of the plans he had made for his own future. John Graves Simcoe's death had been unexpected. She would miss his influence, but she was was capable of looking after her family's interests, and she was not alone. She had many influential friends, and Lord Moira would keep his promise to help Francis as he neared age sixteen.

Part Three

Ensign Francis Simcoe

Chapter 10
Dublin Spring 1808

Francis tells the story of his early months in the British army on two levels. He kept a rather formal journal, factual but lacking anecdote. The events that flesh out his adventures come from the letters he sent to his mother, and his less frequent ones to his sisters. Reading the journal, and comparing it to the more detailed letters echoes a comparison of Elizabeth Simcoe's diary with the more amusing comments sent her by Mary Anne Burges. Like Elizabeth's diary, Francis' journal was meant for a wider audience.

Francis left Eton to spend Christmas at Wolford Lodge, The second since the death of General Simcoe. Mrs. Simcoe entertained many of the village children, but she had neither the spirit nor the strength to produce plays and play host to large numbers of guests. Francis' own thoughts were preoccupied with the future, now upon him. In June 1807, Lord Moira had written Mrs. Simcoe, requesting "the age and Christian name of the son whom you wish to place in the army" and stating his willingness to help. Moira was as good as his word; the War Office acknowledged receipt of the application on 16 July.[1] Francis' commission as Ensign in the 27th (or Inniskilling) Regiment of Foot was signed at Horse Guards on 30 October 1807. The commission cost his mother £400, which was only the beginning of expenses on behalf of her son. Regimentals, a servant, mess bills, and possibly a horse and household goods would add considerably to the costs. Elizabeth agreed to let him have an allowance of £100 a year. On that amount he would be able to pay necessary bills. Even counting his daily pay, he would not be tempted to gamble or drink to excess with his brother officers, both serious vices in the army.

Francis would not be taking up his duties immediately. He had orders not to report to the regimental barracks in Enniskillen until April. (The regiment had kept the archaic spelling of the name.) In the meantime he was far from idle. He was a competent rider, but he resolved to learn to stick to his saddle as well as any cavalryman during a charge. He was also a fair shot with hunting rifle, but he wanted to be as quick as any private at firing a musket. The British infantry prided itself on being able to fire three to four rounds a minute, which required endless hours of practice, perfecting the many movements – priming the pan, dropping in the paper-wrapped charge, pushing it down with the ramrod, returning the rod to the rings on the barrel, and, at last, firing, and immediately reloading. He quickly discovered – as recruits speedily learned – that he could be much faster if he stuck the ramrod in the soil at his feet instead of returning it to the rings, or by thumping the butt hard on the ground.

He also arranged, through his father's former officers, for an instructor in swordsmanship and for a retired officer of the Royal Engineers to help him improve his drafting.

In the library at Wolford Lodge were many of his father's papers, and military manuals. The latter he studied carefully. He found what his mother called Captain John Simcoe's "tracts", and he remembered his father saying that he should study them when he was older. Then he found more of the captain's writings, dated "Cotterstock, Octr. 20th 1754". They were were maxims, written for the edification of his two sons. John Graves was nearly three, and the ill-fated Percy William just over a year old.

There were nineteen altogether, and he asked Eliza if she would have time to make a copy so that he could have it to read after he got settled in Ireland. Number Seven in particular, seemed relevant to the life's work he had chosen:

> Be strenuous in learning your duty, be not afraid of labour or the Tarbucket; but constantly attend, when duty requires you not elsewhere, the boatswain's people in knotting, splicing and rigging, handing and reefing; perfect yourself in the detail of all business from the stem to the stern, from the keelson to the masthead; and learn all duties from the common seaman's to that of the highest commission officer. When you come to be an officer you'll make but an awkward figure, if in ordering the execution of any service you know not how to go about it dextrously yourself; besides such general knowledge in the detail will give you lights and a presence of mind which on occasion may save the Crown's ship or squadron, with the lives of invaluable subjects.[2]

He was moving in the right direction. In this respect a battalion was little different from a ship. Most difficult, but most important was the musket drill. If he could not fire the three rounds a minute, each time replacing the ramrod, how could he stand by while angry sergeants bullied new recruits over their clumsiness? Far better to be able to step forth and demonstrate himself that the army was not demanding the impossible.

Lord Moira invited him to spend a month in London, becoming acquainted and meeting any officers of the regiment who would be there. His Lordship agreed to help him select regimentals, and other equipment he would require. Moira would pay the bills, and submit them to Mrs. Simcoe for repayment, which seemed a satisfactory arrangement to both parties.

Francis left Wolford Lodge by mail coach, in the second week of February, travelling on his own. What budding young officer would risk being delivered to his honorary colonel by his mother, or worse, some of his sisters? He described his journey in a letter dated Tues 15th [February 1808]:

> My dear Mother,
> I arrived here last night after a very long and wearisome journey on account of the badness of the roads, it either rained or snowed the whole of the way. I was introduced to Ensign [George] Lloyd of the 27th with whom I walked a good deal, he came here for a leave of absence as he was shipwrecked a little while ago and narrowly escaped with his life and lost all his baggage.[3]

The 27th Regiment was a large, well-established one. After the Battle of Maida, 6 July 1806, when a 5,100-strong British expedition in Calabria, Italy, defeated a force of more than 6,000 French, the 27th was permitted to count Maida among its battle honours. Francis would be serving with the 3rd Battalion, a new one being raised in Ireland. Of the other two battalions, the 1st was in Italy, and the 2nd at Malta. From the London firm of Ridge, the agent who acted as the regimental banker, Francis heard that promotions in the 27th were rapid "and I from nearly last in the battalion found myself not low in the 2nd."

> I came back to speak to Ld Moira about it who told me that he had leave from the Duke [of York, Commander in Chief] to place the officers in what battalion he liked, and I understood that although I should serve some time in Ireland with the 3d, yet my rank would be going on with the 2d.[4]

Lord Moira had been extremely kind. Francis had a very comfortable room with pens, ink, paper, books. "I admire the breakfast parlour and think it is a very pleasant room it being in the shape of an octagon makes me think it much handsomer." After reporting on various friends, he finished, "You cannot expect a very long letter the first day but you shall have a very long one soon… Best love to all, from your affect. son, F.G. Simcoe. Will be happy to hear from you all."

With an old schoolfellow, Francis attended a play at Drury Lane, a farce on love with a good deal of singing. "I liked it very much." He had called on Mr. Bastard, but had found Mrs. Bastard was unwell. He referred to his father's friend, John Pollexfen Bastard, of Kitley, Devon, who was staying at his London house. Mr. Bastard had written Elizabeth on 6 October, questioning the soundness of Francis' plans. He had heard from William Walcot that the boy was intending to go directly into the army, and had recommended that he first attend a military college, a suggestion Francis rejected.[5]

He went to St. James Church on Sunday morning the 24th, and admired the handsome interior and the fine organ. Afterwards, at dinner, Lord Moira's guests were two titled French exiles, a baron and a duke. The Baron spoke fast, but Francis could understand something of the duke's conversation:

> who is a very pleasant man and not the least like a Frenchman, but the Baron seems a very singluar man. Ld. Moira asked him to drink a glass of wine, and he had just asked for beer, so he took the wine in one hand and the beer in the other, and so drank of one after the other.[6]

Further on in the same letter he wrote, "My regimentals are made and I think I look much better in them than in plain cloathes [sic]." Coats for the 27th were red, faced buff. The rank and file wore tall leather shakos, except for the grenadier company who wore tall bearskin caps. Privates, Sergeants and Corporals wore trousers, white for dress, grey or dark blue for fatigues, and low boots. Officers, except for grenadiers wore cocked hats (the bicornes of the period), white breeches and riding boots or knee-length black gaitors, with white trousers and low boots or shoes for undress. The accoutrements for officers in the 27th were of gold, their sashes of scarlet silk. Such an ensemble was assured to make almost any man look handsome.

On Lord Moira's advice, Francis ordered two sets of regimentals, one dress, the other undress, and some silk hose and a pair of dancing pumps. Because he was growing fast, the tailor made the uniforms with wide seams that could be let out. The coat and breeches did not have quite the cut Francis admired on senior officers, but he did not mind. Once he finished growing would be time enough to look as dashing as possible.

He did not relay any conversations he might have had with Lord Moira concerning his father. Moira must have praised his onetime colleague General Simcoe, but if he did, Francis had no comment to make to his mother. Yet his letters began to hint at a growing respect as the weeks went by. At the same time he always referred to him as "my father", never simply "Father" the way his sisters did.

On 22 February Francis reported on his final visit to Eton, where he packed up his books and arranged to have them sent to Wolford Lodge. "Dr Goodall and my tutor gave me a very handsome book much better than what they usually give for the money that I gave them." He felt rather "out of joints" at taking his last farewell to the college.[7]

The London social life was reminiscent of his mother's in Quebec, with many invitations. In his obvious enjoyment he was more his mother's son than his father's, who had deplored social life in Quebec as frivolous. Francis went to see the British Gallery "where the furnishings were most beautiful." Lord Moira had dined with the Dukes of Gloucestor and Norfolk. Both dukes would be coming to Lord Moira's, but Francis had engaged to dine with one Lord

Rancliffe. "I expect to be very gay next week for I rather think I shall go to the opera and play. Mrs. Bastard is still the same." (Meanwhile, in Upper Canada, the second row of townships along the St. Lawrence River were filling up with settlers. Many went to the township of Burgess, which Simcoe had named for Mary Anne's brother, or to Bastard or Kitley, which honoured John P. The latter's surname had two pronunciations; the family put the emphasis on the second syllable, the residents of Bastard Township on the first. Some may well wonder why the family did not choose a less compromising name.)

On Saturday 5 March, Francis reported visiting the British Museum, and was surprised that he did not have to pay to see the collections. He had dined out and accompanied Lord Moira to the House of Lords. They stayed until nine o'clock in the morning, but Francis was not tired. He had been "much interested in the speeches Ld. Grenville [the prime minister] made." He had called on Colonel Stevenson – Captain Charles Stevenson, his father's deputy quartermaster general in Upper Canada – who introduced him to the Duke of Gloucester "who spoke very kindly of me and made many enquiries after you. We met Ld. Sidmouth [the former Henry Addington] in the street who asked after you." Sidmouth wanted to know when Elizabeth would be coming to London, and he also talked of going to Devon in the summer. At Lord Rancliffe's house Francis had met many Etonians, which helped him feel more at home. He asked his mother whether she had copies of two special books, James' *Military Commission* or James' *Dictionary*, books his father might have acquired. If not he would buy them because an officer needed them.

On Friday 17 March, 1808, Francis wrote from Oundle, in Northamptonshire. He was visiting William Walcot. He had come by coach from Leeds to Stilton, and by post chaise to Oundle. He had left London that morning at eight o'clock and arrived at ten at night. He had ridden with Mr. Walcot to Cotterstock, General Simcoe's birthplace, where he saw the monument in the parish church to Captain John Simcoe, his grandfather. He also rode to Aldwinkle, his mother's birthplace. The country was pretty, with many villages, but not as fine as Devonshire. He had an introductory letter to Sir Edward Littlehales, his father's military secretary in Upper Canada. Littlehales was now a baronet, and the Secretary at War for Ireland with an office in Dublin Castle. Other letters were from Colonel Stevenson and Lord Moira to men of influence who would be useful to Francis.

Later that day, a large dinner party included "Mr. and Mrs. Hunt" who and enquired after the family. He meant Rev. Edward Hunt, son of the Mrs. Ann Hunt who had cared for his sisters during the Canada years, and brother to Miss Mary Hunt, the girls' tutor. When Francis had to take his leave and set out for Ireland, Mr. Walcot lent him his chaise to go twenty miles to Marlborough, where he would take a coach to Holyhead. Before he departed, William Walcot gave him £100 towards his regimental expenses – an enormous sum to entrust to a sixteen-year-old who had never possessed more than a few shillings pocket money.

Francis' journal covers the ground more briefly:

> After spending a month with Lord Moira I left London March 17th 1808, Thursday and travelled in the Liverpool mail as far as Stilton from whence I proceeded to Oundle. Saturday 19th I went thro Northampton & Daventry to Coventry, thence to Lichfield & Chester which latter is a very singular old place. I walked on the wall which surrounds the city & is about 3 m. in circumference. Went to see the Cathedral which is a very indifferent one - from thence I proceeded to Holyhead which I left at two o'clock in the morning of the 23rd & arrived at Dublin at 6 after a very fine & short passage. It is 60 m. across.[9]

In a letter home on 23 March, Francis admitted:

> I was a little seasick and indeed fancy that we are rolling about now. I have been to call on Mr. Wilkinson to whom Ld. Moira gave me a letter, he has been very civil & I dine with him today and go to the play afterwards. Coll Stephenson gve me a letter to Sir Edward Littlehales, on whom I called today, he is going to introduce me to Ld. Harrington and the Duke of of Richmond, he desired his kindest regards to you, that he should do everything in his power to promote my welfare and interest.[10]

Charles Stanhope the 3rd Lord Harrington was commander in chief of troops in Ireland. Charles Lennox the 4th Duke of Richmond was the Lord Lieutenant. Sir Edward, who had played with Francis as a child, asked him to have his letters directed "under cover" through his office at Dublin Castle. Elizabeth should mark "private" on the cover "He being Secretary at War would always know where [my regiment] was." It would not be the least trouble and he would be very vexed if they did not. Lady Elizabeth, Sir Edward's wife, had just been confined with a daughter.

He expected to dine "tomorrow" with Sir Edward, and to have breakfast with Joseph Atkinson, to whom he carried a letter from Lord Moira. Atkinson had served as a lieutenant under Rawdon/Moira in the Volunteers of Ireland, and he remembered Colonel Simcoe and his Queen's Rangers very well. He drew half-pay as a lieutenant although he had had a captaincy in a later regiment.[11]

"I think I will stay a week in Dublin as I am not to be with my regiment until the 10th of April". The scenery had been very grand through Wales over the mountains. Thus far he had found the public buildings of Dublin very handsome. "You shall hear from me very constantly; Give my best to my Sisters, Henry and friends. Believe me ever faithfully F.G. Simcoe."

From London, on 25 March, Lord Moira sent Elizabeth the bills for "our young soldier's" outfits for which he had paid.[12] As Francis would find out later, his mother was alarmed at how much money had been spent.

On the same day, Francis was writing that he had dined with Mr. Atkinson, and had gone to plays with him, "The Earl of Essex" and the farce "The Midnight Hour". The theatre was very pretty but small, and the actors indifferent. Apparently Atkinson did not admit that he was a dramatist with several works to his name or Francis would have noted it. He remarked again on Dublin's handsome public buildngs. The streets were wide but badly paved, and the houses small. "Irish money differs very much from English, and I find I may get a shilling every pound by my money which is English."

He had attended a grand route given by the Duke and Duchess of Richmond. He had gone with Sir Edward Littlehales. Sir Charles Vernon introduced him to the Duke and Duchess, and Sir Edward to Lord Harrington with whom Francis dined the following Sunday. That dinner followed the Duke's levee at two o'clock in the afternoon, where he was impressed with the profusion of diamonds. "I was introduced to a great number of officers who served under my father and were very pleased to see me." He also met Lady Bilmore "and many other Ladies of rank." Lady Bilmore and her husband lived near Enniskillen and she was first cousin to Lord Enniskillen, to whom Sir Edward Littlehales had given Francis a letter of introduction. "There were three large rooms, one opening into the other, all very much crowded, there were near 500 people but it was called a small party. " He dined with the provost of the college of Dublin, whom he had met at the Castle. Sir Edward Littlehales had very excellent apartments there, and a fine country house known as Phoenix Park, which he would soon show to Francis. Sir Edward asked him to consider him his best friend.[13]

The next letter is dated Dublin, Monday April 5th 1808. He was pleased to receive a letter, which had been delayed by contrary winds. If Elizabeth were to see Lord Harrington while in London, or others who had been kind, would she express her thanks? He often dined or breakfasted with Lord Harrington, and rode out with young ladies of his very pleasant family of four sons and two daughters. The Harringtons generously offered him the use of a horse.

He rode, too, to the Littlehales residence, Phoenix Park, with grounds eight miles in circumference. The view was beautiful, as it looked down on Dublin, the Liffey River and the mountains of Wicklow. He played chess with Lady Anne Maria Stanhope, elder daughter of Lord Harrington. "The Duchess of Richmond has taken a great deal of notice of me." Some may wonder what Francis meant by "notice". The party-giving Duchess might have had an eye for pleasant youngsters fresh from their celebate public schools.

The Duke of Richmond, Lord Lieutenant of Ireland, was a colourul man who, when a captain of the Coldstream Guards in 1789, had challenged the Duke of York to a duel. Fellow officers later declared that Lennox had acted with courage but not judgement. He succeeded to the dukedom in December 1806. The year before Francis Simcoe arrived in Dublin, Colonel Sir Arthur Wellesley, was serving as Richmond's Chief Secretary. Sir Arthur, until he redeemed himself in India, had been regarded as the least promising of the sons of Lord Mornington. Francis would serve under the future Duke of Wellington in the Peninsula.

In his letter Francis reminded his mother of her friendship with Thomas Talbot, the governor's aide de camp in Upper Canada:

> "I have dined twice with Mrs. Talbot, the mother of your friend who is very civil to me. She has some daughters, very pretty girls ... I went with Mrs. T. and Miss T. to a drawingroom and was surprised at how ladies with hoops sat on the same side of the coach. I hardly thought there was room.[14]

For the occasion Francis had worn full regimentals. He also met Lady St. George, the grandmother of Elizabeth Lady Littlehales. "This is a very extraordinary old woman near 90 and all faculties perfectly etc. ... Tell my sisters they can help themselves to any book of mine except the poets Virgil, Homer and Horace, as keepsakes of my affection."

On Thursday, 8 April, the night before he left Dublin to join his regiment, Francis attended the Duchess of Richmond's "large party" at Dublin Castle. About 300 people were there, and most danced. The Castle was magnificent, and everybody was elegantly dressed, the supper magnificent. He returned "home" to his lodgings at three a.m. Perhaps, on all the occasions when the Duchess was taking notice, Sir Edward Littlehales kept an attentive eye. Perhaps he made certain that all invitations issued to his young friend were to her Grace's larger functions. When a still quite sleepy Francis boarded the mail coach for Enniskillen, he was carrying a letter from Littlehales to the temporary commander of the 3rd Battalion 27th (or Inniskilling) Foot, Major William Brydges Neynoe.

Chapter 11

At Enniskillen with the Inniskillings

Francis gave a brief description of his introduction to Enniskillen in his journal:

April 9th left Dublin & arrived at Enniskillen on the 10th after a very tiresome & fatiguing journey in the mail which never travels at above 4. an hour. We were 22 hours going 80 Irish m. which is nearly 100 English. Here I joined the 3rd Battalion of the 27th Reg't (Maida) as 2d Ensign so that I have not to carry the Colours. Major [William Brydges] Neynoe commands the Batt. Capt. [George] Humphrey my company.[1]

Officially a line company consisted of 100 privates and non-commissioned officers, one captain, one lieutenant and one ensign. For a regiment on active service the number of privates might be fifty or even less. When Francis arrived at Enniskillen, his name was on a list of "supernumerary or officers en second".[2] Other items on the lists of officers shed light on how the the army operated. Lord Moira's rank as colonel was an honorary one. The lieutenant colonel who actually commanded the battalion was John Maclean. Each battalion had ten companies, which operated in two wings, each under a major. Of the ten companies, eight were "of the line." The Light Company, positioned at the left end of the line of battle, was of skirmishers. The Grenadier Company, on the right of the line companies, was of men who stood a minimum of six feet tall in their boots or shoes, and were intended to give strength in a push. Both the Light and Grenadier companies were the elite of the battalion. Placed on the flanks, they protected the most vulnerable positions. In their tall, bearskin hats, Grenadiers tended to attract admiring attention. The commander of Grenadiers was likely to be the senior captain in the battalion.

One major was Charles Thompson, the other was Peter Nicholson, but both were absent. The two majors Francis met were supernumeraries. Major Neynoe was acting temporarily as brigade major; Lieutenant Colonel Maclean was also absent. When Francis went to report to Major Neynoe, he found that Major John Birmingham was in charge of the whole battalion. In the absence of Major Neynoe, Francis handed the letter Sir Edward Littlehales had entrusted to him to Major Birmingham, who opened it.

Once he was assigned lodgings near the barracks, Francis took out the maxims – nineteen in all – that Captain John Simcoe had prepared in 1754, when his son John Graves was under three years old. It was entitled "Rules For Your Conduct". Number one read:

> Let the groundwork of your whole conduct be a just respect for and love of God; know that with such intent every man necessarily be brave, and without such due impression every man must as necessarily be a coward.[3]

Others stressed love of country and King, the essential principle of Honour, never to forget that he was a servant of the Public. Other than number seven, on being able to do any job around a ship, which Francis had taken to heart back at Wolford Lodge, five and six seemed the most significant:

> 5. Let your obedience to the command of Superior Officers be exact, implicit and cheerful; if those commands should at any time be indiscreet, or lead you instantly to sudden death you are in all cases most punctually to execute them and know the first virtue in an inferior is cheerful obedience and – hesitation, impiety – your superior alone being answerable for his orders.

> 6. He who knows not how to obey, can never know how to command; you are therefore not only to obey promptly and with all your spirit the commands of a Superior but you are in the course of your service to learn practically the distinct duties of every officer.

The words were his grandfather's, yet he could hear his father's voice as he read them. They were not very comforting to a brand new ensign facing his first duty, but Francis could see that they made sense. The army was not unlike Eton. The wayward junior boy was never the one who was made a prefect, nor was he respected by his fellows. He reread number five. If he were given an incompetent order, could he obey it if he knew it meant certain death, not just to himself, but to inferiors who placed their trust in him?

At first, Francis felt very strange. As an extra ensign, he disliked the feeling that his place in Captain Humphrey's company was temporary. He found settling in difficult when he did not know how long he would be there. Suddenly, he knew what he really wanted. He had measured himself and standing tall he had reached the magic height of six feet in his stocking feet. The captain of the Grenadier Company was John Tucker, but, he was away in Malta, serving as the captain for the grenadiers in the 2nd Battalion. This made a vacancy in the Grenadier Company of the 3rd Battalion a certainty, and, Francis knew the man most likely to be receive the captaincy. Lieutenant John Pring was also from Honiton, and the Simcoe and Pring families were well acquainted. John's commission as a lieutenant in the 27th dated from 31 March 1804. After four years as a subaltern, Pring had the seniority for the promotion. If

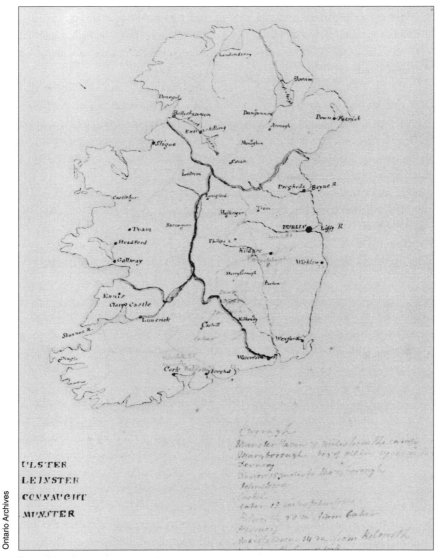

Map of the Irish provinces drawn by Francis Simcoe.

Pring was to be the captain of Grenadiers, Francis hoped he would be sent to his company.

Pring was in luck; he received command of the Grenadiers as acting captain, although it would be temporary until Horse Guards sent permission. Pring might have to pay £950. A captaincy cost £1,500, but he could sell his lieutenancy for £550, which would cover the difference. Traditionally, apart from having the wealth to purchase, another way to achieve promotion in an infantry regiment was in the field, or by joining a brand new regiment. A field promotion rested on demonstrating courageous leadership. Commissions in a new regiment were free, because rules forbad selling commissions before a battalion reached full strength.

By the time Francis had joined the army, because of reforms in the system, awarding commissions without purchase was becoming more common. An officer who had shown competence might not have to pay, as long as he had seniority. Soldiers from the ranks might win commissions by displaying exceptional talent. Whereas commissions for men from the ranks had once been about one in twenty, commissions without purchase to line officers, especially for the Light Infantry, amounted to upwards of seventeen percent. Light infantrymen were learning to operate as individuals. Battalion companies and Grenadiers were expected to keep their positions and act in unison.

Francis knew that he was privileged, and he wondered, if he had been low born, whether he would have had the ability to rise if he had had to start as a "ranker".

Gaining a lieutenancy by purchase would not be difficult. Being promoted captain was much harder, even when there was money for purchase. A company might have more than one lieutenant, just as it could have more than one ensign, but a company required the leadership of just one man. For any aspiring officer, the captaincy was the first real step towards a successful career, towards reaching high rank as his father had done. John Graves Simcoe's captaincy had been by purchase, in the 40th Foot, but he had won his majority by sheer bravery and competence in the field, and all subsequent promotions had been on merit – or the influence of politicians such as Lord Sidmouth, or Lord Moira.

Writing home on 11 April, Francis told Elizabeth that a Colonel Windham, the commander of a detachment of the Royals, who were quartered at the barracks, had asked after her. "I don't remember seeing him before nor did I know that you had." His tone was dry; he was finding Windham's men rather noisy. Lough Erne was very beautiful, but he did not expect to stay long at Enniskillen, perhaps a fortnight. The battalion would be going on exercises in the field. He had tolerable lodgings, but they were not cheap, and he was very busy getting settled in.[4]

He had scarcely sealed this letter and taken it to the post when he received a letter from Elizabeth. He replied immediately, feeling as though the roof had caved in. He was surprised that she mentioned his "immense stock of cloathes."

> I assure you that you are much mistaken. I had no more than what was really necessary and that Ld. Moira's own desire. I had but two suits of regimentals and whatever else I had Ld. Moira approved of, and told me I could not do with less.

Only in the matter of boots had he been extravagant, but even then Lord Moira agreed, as "elsewhere I might not get boots to fit except at great inconvenience." He had to admit that he had encountered heavier expenses than he expected. His regimentals, sword, cocked hat, etc. had cost more than he thought they would. When Elizabeth went to London, Lord Moira could show her the bills, and if she still felt that he had overspent needlessly, "let me know and I will try to pay it out of my own pocket." There was faint chance of that; an ensign's pay in an infantry regiment was four shillings and eightpence a day. Even though he was entitled to allowances for special expenditures, this was far from enough to cover basic expenses.[5] As well, the journey to Ireland had cost more than the £20 they both had thought sufficient, and did not cover the cost of the fortnight in Dublin.[6]

The following day he wrote again, after he received another letter from Elizabeth, dated 14 March under cover from Lord Moira whose frank was dated 14 April – two days after he received it.

> I do not know whether you understood I meant to make use of Mr. Walcot's £100 paying for my equipment and journey, supposing it would entirely for both, but since it would not pay for more than my cloathes and partly that, I thought myself justifiable in claiming from Ld. Moira money to pay for my journey and I took the 100 which you was to allow me yearly, as I thought I should want part of it when I arrived here, and it would save a deal of trouble which it would have cost me to have it remitted to me here, so that when you paid the £121, 10, 0 to Ld Moira you will be nothing more to give me this year.[7]

Major Neynoe had returned, and Francis had been introduced to him. General James Affleck, the commander of the district, was expected soon. "I find that we pay 13 shillings for our dinners which I think very reasonable, especially as we get very good ones… wine is not included on the dinner, but that does not come to a great deal as it is only between 2d and 3d per bottle." His servant, who belonged to the regiment and had been assigned to him, would cost 2s 6d to 3s 6d weekly. Except for dinners the officers took all their meals at their own lodgings.

I do not know whether you have my grandfather's military tracts, my
Father often desired me that I should read them when I was old enough,
and he always said that they were the greatest treasure he ever possessed.
If you think there was any chance of their being lost, I would not wish
them to be sent, but otherwise I would. If you was to send them to Sir
Edward Littlehales they would go free and I think he never knew a letter
to miscarry which was sent to him since he had been in office.[8]

He closed with, "Best love to all at Wolford, Ashfield, Egland etc, and
likewise to Henry. When you write tell Henry I shall certainly write to him.
Your dutiful son F.G. Simcoe" Ashfield, about the same distance from Wolford
Lodge as Tracey, was Mary Anne Burges' new home. Egland belonged to
Misses Frances Anne and Mary Elliott, daughters of an admiral who were dear
friends of both Elizabeth and Mary Anne.

Before many weeks had passed Francis was able to read Captain John
Simcoe's tracts. His sisters settled down most willingly to copy out everything
their adored brother requested. Making copies was a constant chore. At least
four handwritten copies of Elizabeth's Canadian diary are in the Ontario
Archives. Many Simcoe letters from various periods are in more than one
hand. (The most readable version of Francis' Irish journal is in a hand clearer
than his own.)

Drill occupied the battalion constantly. On Mondays and Fridays they
held Battalion Drill; Thursdays and Saturdays were for Brigade Drill; Wednes-
days were Field Days; Thursdays were a Day of Rest. The men drilled two or
three times a day, ordered about by the NCOs. Once they mastered the intricate parade ground drill (which they would repeat on the battlefield) they proceeded to musket drill.[9] While the sergeants commanded the drill, officers had
to be on hand to supervise, and to ascertain that the NCOs were not too hard on
the men.

Next came drills for forming the hollow square, infantry's best defence
against cavalry. With bayonets fixed onto the ends of muskets, butts braced on
the ground and slanting outwards, the sight alone would cause horses to veer
away. The sergeant major, company sergeant majors and sergeants, the drill-
masters, were not satisfied until the men could form square in one minute.

On 14 April Francis wrote that the weather was still very cold in
Enniskillen. "They say there is little summer here. It is certainly very dull at
present ... but I believe this is the dullest part of the year." Some of the battalion might be sent to Ballyshannon, where quarters were much worse. The battalion now had 1,000 men. An officer recruiting at Sligo brought in 100 men,
but a sergeant found 500. The strangeness was passing, "I shall soon get into
the way of it. The officers are very civil to me."[10]

Ten days later, Sunday the 24th, he had received Elizabeth's letter of the
11th but could not respond sooner because of being "extremely unwell for the

past week with a terrible cold, with headache and sore throat, but thank God I am very much recovered." Many of the officers said they were ill. Elizabeth had written that she had postponed going to London, and he was sorry because now she would have to endure the heat of summer in the city. Great Aunt Margaret Graves was beginning to fail, which was sad news. He was glad to hear that eight-year-old Henry was liking school. Francis had written to him, and hoped he would reply "if he can find time." Elizabeth had asked him for sketches of the countryside, but he had not been well enough to make any:

> "I assure you your little sketches soon, scenes around here are very pretty, will write pleasanter letters once I will be in better spirits. Best to all, remember me to Miss Burges, Julia and Miss Elliott when you see them.[11]

On 6 May, Sir Edward Littlehales wrote to Elizabeth from Phoenix Park. He was enquiring about the status of military lands – mainly the 200 acres on which Castle Frank had been built –that had been left to Francis by "his revered father". He had not heard from Francis for some time, but had received a good account from Lord Bilmore. Littlehales was anxious to be of service to the whole Simcoe family because of the respect he held for General Simcoe's memory.[12]

Francis wrote to his mother the same day. He was often unwell, and had not had time to make the promised sketches. His days were very full of duties. The weather had turned very hot, which did not help. He had at last been introduced to General Affleck, who had been very kind, and who recalled serving under General Simcoe in San Domingo. Captain Humphrey, his company commander, was a very good officer, and an agreeable man and very kind to him. Officers of all levels seemed pleased to meet him. The positive reaction was partly a tribute to his father, but also owing to Francis' own eagerness to learn his job and to the competence he was showing. The branch was proving as solid as the tree.

Most of the fish from Lough Erne, he reported, were very bad, but they had had some nice perch and fine salmon from Ballyshannon, on the Shannon River system which extended to within thirty miles of Enniskillen. "Please present the enclosed to Catherine [sic] as I am exceeding obliged for her pretty letter, glad she can write so well". Katherine was now seven years old, and being pushed as hard as the other children at her lessons. "I understand we are to have another field day tomorrow; much rain, the ground on which we are to be reviewed is quite a bog." He knew he would be tired out after five or six hours out.[13]

By 24 May, a Tuesday, he reported nothing but field days for more than three weeks. He longed for a horse to carry him home after the long days of heavy exertion:

I had for part of the time command of my Company as my Captain and Senior Subaltern were absent and the whole command devolved upon myself. We are still very busy preparing for camp for which we begin our march on Monday next. Genl Affleck and Major Neynoe both wished me and the officers who are to remain here as my health has been indifferent, but I believe it arose from nothing but fast growth and taking a great deal of exercise as I measure six foot and a quarter in my boots and I think you will find me much altered when we meet again.

He had come very near to getting into the Grenadiers, which he wanted very much but he was not sure whether he would or not. "I am to my great sorrow ordered to another company which I regret much as I liked my Captain exceedingly." Being in camp, he warned Elizabeth to forestall further criticism, would be very expensive. Officers had allowances for many things, but no camp allowance, and would have to find everything for themselves. He finished the letter on Friday the 27th:

I have just been put in the Grenadiers which I am not sorry for as the officers in the Company know their duty perfectly, and I am likely to learn my duty to my Captain as any off in the regiment. He has also seen a good deal of service.

He did not mention John Pring by name, probably because his mother already knew, from the captain's own mother, that he had acting command of the Grenadier Company. Francis regretted having so little time to write. The officers had received the route "today and we march on Monday at 1 o'clock in the morning to be at Curragh [camp] the 6th of June which is my birthday. The distance from here is about 130 miles." Apparently his health had improved sufficiently for him to accompany the battalion. He would be leaving Enniskillen at a beautiful time of year and would never return. In closing he asked Elizabeth to Excuse the shameful scribble. He had hardly five minutes to write while eating breakfast.[14]

The army was preparing to embark for Portugal or Spain, to protect the Portuguese from Napoleon's marshals, and to accept the Spanish, formerly the enemy, as allies. Sir Arthur Wellesley, appointed lieutenant general on 25 April, would shortly be leading an expeditionary force to Portugal to reinforce the commander of the British army in the Peninsula, Sir John Moore. The march Francis was shortly to begin was from Enniskillen to the Cove of Cork, where transport vessels were concentrating to carry troops and supplies.

Francis wrote nothing about conditions that existed in Ireland. He had moved among the Anglo-Irish gentry, for the most part shielded from the evidence of widespread poverty. Under the Protestant ascendency, the Gaelic-speaking Catholic peasants sheltered in hovels beside their subsistence potato patches. Their lives were more squalid than among similarly badly off people in rural Devonshire. Landlords were generally Protestant, although a few Catholic land owners had managed to keep their estates. The birth rate was high and families were large. Rents were exorbitantly high for small holders, and many landless cottars worked on the estates of the elite for wages that would barely support their families. The potato famine of the 1840s was already a disaster waiting to happen.

The Irish had rebelled in 1798 – when General Simcoe had taken command of troops in the West Country in anticipation of interference from France. One of the most rebellious parts had been Ulster, despite a better economy, higher standard of living and a Protestant majority. Some time before, Pitt, as prime minister, had mooted Catholic emancipation and union with Great Britain as a solution to the Irish problem. What the Irish got, following the rebellion, was union, without Catholic emancipation.

Poverty, rather than any principle, sent young men flocking to enlist when recruiting agents came near. Whole regiments were filled with Irish soldiers, as was the 27th. Whereas the rank and file were largely Protestant, many other regiments were filled with Catholics except for most of the commissioned officers. One of the most effective regiments was the 88th Connaught Rangers, men almost uncontrollable as drunken rioters in camp or off duty, but in battle they were the best troops in the British army.

Chapter 12

The March from Enniskillen to the Cove of Cork

Francis wrote that the battalion would be rising at one o'clock on the morning of Monday 30 May. They were making an early start. The normal time for reveille was an hour and a half before dawn. The men required an hour before they could be ready to march. NCOs had to see that the men were fully dressed. Staff sergeants were responsible for seeing that all baggage was packed. A captain was permitted three tons of baggage, which made Francis smile. He had not had time to accumulate many worldly goods, so that his amounted to less than one ton. His duty as a subaltern was to inspect the company, to make sure that the NCOs had been thorough. He had to examine all the muskets to make certain that locks worked, and that each soldier had good flints. Their cartridge cases were empty; ammunition would not be issued until they were preparing for a campaign.

To be on the safe side he ordered each man to fire his weapon to prove that none of the barrels were gummed up with old powder. The battalion formed up, in four files where the road was wide, or two where it was too narrow. On the move, majors marched behind their wings, captains behind their companies. Because Lieutenant Colonel Maclean had not yet joined the battalion, Major Neynoe was in command, and Major Birmingham walked in the rear. With the adjutant, Neynoe rode up and down inspecting the column. The baggage train, the officers' extra horses, the servants, and the mule train carrying extra ammunition and biscuit (hard tack that kept well) followed the column. Then came the battalion women – five men in each company were allowed to bring their wives to do the housekeeping, the mending, washing, and meal preparation for the enlisted men. If they had children, they were tagging along. Once the battalion had left camp, men of the Provost Marshal's staff, the army's police, went over the ground, rounding up stragglers. When they completed their search the Provosts followed the others.

The colour party marched in the middle of the column, between the 4th and 5th battalion companies. The Light and Grenadier Companies were not numbered. One colour, the King's, was the Union Jack with the regimental number in the centre. The other, the regimental or second colour, was buff, the same as the facings on the coats, with a small Union Jack in the upper right corner. Two ensigns bore the flags, flanked by the colour sergeants carrying their nine-foot pikes. In a battle the sergeants would guard the colours if the enemy got too close; at all costs the foe must not be permitted to capture them.

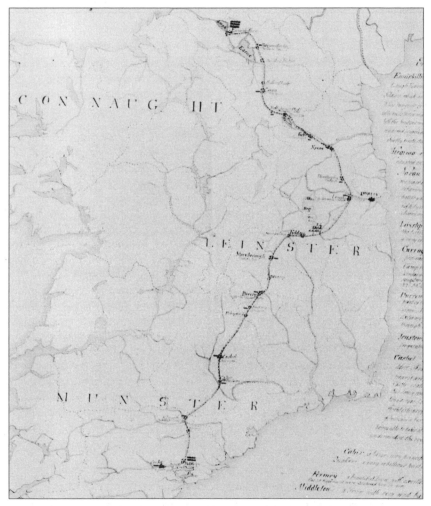

Ontario Archives

Francis Simcoe drew maps and marked his route, both in Ireland and while campaigning in Spain and Portugal.

The battalion was accustomed to stopping half an hour into the march for breakfast, for which everyone was ready after the exercise of packing up and starting out. Francis had drawn a detailed map of the route, but many places named on it or mentioned in his journal are now very small, or have had their names changed since the partition of Ireland:

> 30th. we left Enniskillen & marched to Maguires Bridge. 31st. from thence through New Town, Butler, & Butler's Bridge to Cavan. June 1st. left Cavan & marched to thru Bally James Duff to Virginia, a small but beautiful town situated on Lake Ramor. 2nd. left Virginia & marched to Kells.[1]

At Kells (now called Ceanannus Mòr) he had time for a quick letter. He was sorry for being unable to write sooner, but preparations for camp had taken up much time. He had written one letter, but it accidently got packed in his trunk and taken to the baggage train before he could retrieve it. Today's march had been mercifully short:

> I must say my feet are rather hurt and blistered, but my being in the Grenadiers forbids me to talk of such trifles. Norwithstanding my ill health of late, I assure you I think you will hardly know me when I see you next as I have something like a colour in my face I do not at all dislike.[2]

He expected to have a lot of "hard and fagging duty" but he felt able to cope. "Sir David Baird is to command." General Baird was to lead 10,000 reinforcements being gathered at Curragh Camp and other points farther south. When this army reached Spain, Baird would be second in command to Sir John Moore, who with only 20,000 troops was attempting to dislodge the French from central Spain.

Francis' journal continued:

> 3rd [June] Marched through Navan within 2 m. of which we passed over the the Bridge of the Boyne so famous on account of the battle gained there by K. William in 1690. The Soldiers gave three cheers on passing the Bridge.

> 4th. marched to Leixslip, a most beautiful town on the Liffey 7 m. from Dublin. [Leixslip is not on modern maps.] This is a very rebellious part of the Country. I was billeted with three other officers at a Col. Morley's who has a most beautiful place & treated us sumptuously. Indeed you may everywhere see the native hospitality of the Irish. 6th. arrived at Curragh famous for being the first race ground in Europe; after an extremely long & fatiguing march. We set out at 8 o'clock at night & arrived at 10 in the morning. We were the first Reg't that marched into Camp, the forming of which was a very fine sight. 6 or 8 Regiments came in within an hour of one another & at given signal within 5 minutes every Tent on the ground was pitched. The Regiments who formed the

camp consisted of one Troop of Horse, Artillery, several squadrons of Cavalry commanded by Genl Affleck, 1st Royals, 23rd, 26th, 27th, 30th, 48th, 66th, 81st & several Militia Reg'ts.

Monday 6 June was Francis' seventeenth birthday. On Wednesday, he wrote to his mother from Curragh. He had posted the letter from his trunk, but had misplaced a sketch he had made. He was feeling better every day, and would soon be able to march as well as any officer in the regiment:

> I like the Grenadiers very much although it was rather expensive in the new company as we wear 2 epaulettes instead of one, and a sabre instead of a sword, and an handsome cap. When I am a little settled you shall have a larger and more entertaining letter. We have a very pretty view of Kildare. … Tell Eliza am much obliged for her letter. More reg'ts arrived today.[3]

His news was not quite what he admitted, because he had to pay for two epaulettes of costly gold thread. All ranks of Grenadiers had "wings" along the shoulder seams of their jackets. His battalion company epaulette would not fit over the wings the tailors had sewn on his red coat. His old sword had been long; the sabre was shorter and lighter. The handsome cap replaced the officer's cocked hat of the battalion companies. The cap had regimental badge in gold in front, regimental number on the back, and was made high with bearskin. It added some ten inches to his height, but was not as high nor as heavy as the busby worn by modern Grenadier Guards.

He wrote again on Sunday the 12th. His friend Joseph Atkinson had written to General Byngham [Bingham], the Commander of Brigades, recommending Ensign Simcoe as a capable young officer. The general, who was very civil to Francis, remembered serving under General Simcoe in San Domingo. Francis' greatest inconvenience was not having a horse, for it was difficult to find a good one. He wanted to be able to ride back after having a strenuous field day. He thought he would be well able to afford a mount in another year. The Duke of Richmond and Lord Harrington would be coming to review the troops soon. He hoped Sir Edward Littlehales would be accompanying them.

They remained at Curragh Camp for nearly seven weeks, during which the regiments drilled as constantly as the 27th had while in Enniskillen. Here Francis would certainly have witnessed punishment parades. With so many troops concentrated, infractions of rules were inevitable because not all the battalions comprised troops who were easy to discipline. A battalion would be drawn up on three sides of the parade square. On the open side, a triangle formed from sergeants' pikes would have been erected, where for quite minor offenses, a stripped soldier would be tied and flogged. All officers serving in the battalion had to be present, and many from other regiments came as well.

If any deserters were captured, the routine was even more sickening. The battalion would be drawn up as for floggings, but this time the captive would be tied to a tree or post along the open side, a wooden coffin close by. Then the firing party marched over. Muskets were not very accurate. Too often the shots did not kill, and the Provost Marshal would march forward and finish the execution with his pistol. Francis did not mention attending such horrific events, for they were hardly something he would write to his mother about. Nor would he put in a journal details that would offend the sensibilities of his sisters, Miss Burges or Julia Somerville.

From what Francis wrote about officers of the 27th, floggings must have been rare and desertion from the battalion uncommon. The men in the ranks had enlisted voluntarily, and responded positively to efficient but fair treatment. The officers were competent professionals, and capable of controlling their men without recourse to the sadistic cruelty allowed under military law. As Francis had told Elizabeth, he could learn from the officers of Grenadiers as well as from any in the army.

By 6 July Francis had acquired a horse. He had to pay thirty guineas for it, but he could not get one for much less. He also bought a "pretty little tent", necessary because the government was going to take back the camp tents and give the officers an allowance for them. Then he exchanged the tent he bought for a smaller one that was lined and warmer.[4] Even in summer Ireland was not balmy at night.

On the 21st, the Duke of Richmond came and reviewed the regiments. Afterwards they received the route for a march to Middleton (now Midleton) Barracks, which were close to the Cove of Cork. There they would remain until transports were available to take them to Spain. Francis' journal resumed:

> 22nd. left the Curragh at 4 in the morning. We march in two Divisions, the 2nd Division marches tomorrow from the camp. Every Battalion is divided into 10 companies, 1050 Comps are in each Div. The Grenadiers, Band, Colors [sic] & Staff always go together so that I came with the 1st Div. We breakfasted at Munsterhaven about 8 m. from the Camp near which is a castle on a high rock which has a very grand appearance. Leaving Kildare we entered the most beautiful & highly cultivated country & arrived at Marysborough.

As with his father's Queen's Rangers, the 27th had two types of band. Military instruments were the fifes and drums of the infantry, and the bugles of the cavalry. The officers' Band of Music played a variety of brass and woodwind instruments. When the battalion was in column, the Band of Music marched along the flank. Each fifer and drummer marched with his own company.

On 23 July Francis' regiment again marched at four in the morning. The road was fine until they came to a small part of the great bog of Allen which they marched through. Soon afterwards they arrived at Devaney, a small village. They received a note from Lord Devaney "whose domain lies close to the village to pass through his grounds". This shortened the route by two miles. They marched close to his house and through a lovely wood. "The lofty hedges & fine trees put me put me in mind of Devonshire."

They halted at Marysborough and resumed their march on the 24th, through Johnstown, a spa, and Urlingford. On the 26th they reached Cashel, "a large dirty town the oldest Archbishoprick [sic] in Ireland." Near it lay the ruins of a magnificent castle seated on an immense rock. The town had once belonged to the Archbishop of Cashel. Far back in the past, a certain Earl laid siege to the castle, and when he could not take it by storm he undermined the rock and blew it up. On the 27th they reached Cahir, "a large town principally inhabited by Quakers, a very rebellious part of the country." They stopped at Kilworth, a very dirty town, "the worst I have yet seen."

> 30th. arrived at Middleton Barracks between which & Kilworth is the beautiful and neat town of Fermoy in which are excellent Barracks. The 20th Reg't which left the Curragh with us is quartered here & also the Royals at Cork. Middleton Barracks are much larger & handsomer than Enniskillen, the town very small & neat about 7 m. from Kilworth.

The battalion would remain at Middleton Barracks until 13 September. The last item in his journal read, "Aug. 22. Lt. Col. [John] Maclean has joined and taken the command of the Regiment. He is very gentlemanlike and has seen a great deal of service." [5]

Early in August Francis rode to Cork to satisfy his curiosity about the port. On his return he sold his horse, for thirty guineas, the amount he had paid for it. He could have got more, but did not feel right about exploiting another officer. Rumours abounded in the barracks. A favourite was that the Duke of York would be commanding this "immense expedition". He appreciated Sir Edward Littlehales, who was still faithfully forwarding the letters from home. Francis had not seen him, for he had remained in Dublin when the Duke of Richmond inspected the troops. [6] Several letters he wrote from Middleton are too faint to read today, but his last, dated 13 September is legible. He caught the last post before sailing. They were to embark by Monday, the 18th and sail on Tuesday. The 27th Regiment would accompany the Royals, 23rd, 25th, and 31st. His battalion was 800 strong, but they were leaving about 300 behind under a new major. They would pay for their tents from an embarkation allowance. The transports would be calling at Falmouth for 2,000 more troops.

Loading so many troops aboard all the transports took many days. On 8 September Sir David Baird received an order to begin the march to the Cove of Cork from the various barracks at five o'clock the next morning, "wherefore on the 9th we proceeded:

It happened to fall upon my lot to command the baggage guard. There
was a ferry; it was necessary to pass over before we could arrive at Cove.
Accordingly the Regiment went over on boats as it was 3 or 4 miles
down the river to the harbour where the transports lay. The Regiment
proceeded ... but the baggage went down the river in boats. As I commanded the guard I went with it. We had a most beautiful view down the
river and arrived in the harbour where I embarked the baggage on board
the different ships as it had been a long time since I had been on board
any ship, never so small as a transport, it was quite new to me.[7]

He was surprised after being embarked, to find that eleven officers, two
women and two children were sharing a cabin where they had hardly room to
move. This he found extraordinary that two women would insist on following
their husbands under such conditions. Just two small partitions separated the
women from the men. "They were obliged to go through our cabin if they
wished to go out of their own":

Cove is a very pretty little town. The harbour is a most beautiful one.
During my stay at this place which far exceeded my expectations
[because of the length of it], I took a trip to Cork by water. It is about 6
miles distance, and I was much pleased with myself. The river is very
beautiful and picturesque...I likewise went to see a beautiful castle
which commanded the harbour ... At last the transports removing with
the artillery on the 19th... The staff officers' horses were embarked on
the 23rd of September.

According to barracks gossip, Sir Hugh Dalrymple and Sir Arthur Wellesley were to be advanced to the peerage. Wellesley would be, but not until September 1809. As for Dalrymple, he had been sent to take command in Spain, to
be superior to Sir John Moore. Dalrymple was a doddering old fool who had
not seen a battlefield for years. He was an old friend of the Simcoe and Burges
families but that did not make him worthy of the task. Francis wrote again on
the 20th and the 22nd, aboard the transport vessel *Tyne*. The fleet, of sixty sail
of transports, was waiting for wind.

After five days at sea, and buffeting autumn gales, he reached Falmouth by Thursday 29 September, and wrote to his "Dearest Family". He
was glad all were well except Mrs. Graves, who continued to fail. He
thought the troops might be some time in Falmouth, or they might move on
to Plymouth. The rest of the letter was garbled. He was clearly upset by
events in Portugal. Bonaparte seemed to be "taking it very easy" ... I can't
find anything glorious in the late intervention. French in English vessels
with arms, ammunition and plunder and lay waste to the country seems
extraordinary."

He was fuming over the Cintra Convention signed in Portugal on 31 August, for which Sir Hugh Dalrymple was responsible. In July, Sir Arthur Wellesley had been sent in command of an expeditionary force to Portugal. In August he had defeated the French at Rolica and Vimeiro. When Dalrymple arrived, superceding Wellesley, he agreed to an utterly stupid arrangement whereby the captured French would be allowed to depart in ships of the Royal Navy Squadron based at Lisbon instead of being held as prisoners of war. Outrage in Britain as immediate because the troops would undoubtedly be sent to join the French army in Spain, which was already threatening Sir John Moore's force. Wellesley, who had wanted to continue driving the French out of Portugal, had been recalled to face a Court of Inquiry. At Horse Guards the generals had left Sir John Moore in command of the army while they discussed who would be a suitable successor to Dalrymple.

Francis admitted that he was happy to be back in England, despite having enjoyed his time in Ireland:

> I understand that we were to wait ... for 5000 cavalry who were expected to join us... While staying in Falmouth Harbour I went to Pendennis and Maws Castle[s]. It was so long since I had been at Pendennis that I almost forgot it. A small brig in which a part of our Regiment were aboard which happened to lie behind was not able to get into the harbour and was driven by contrary winds into Plymouth, however it joined us before we left Falmouth which was on the 9th of October with our 160 sail of transports for Corunna.

They left Falmouth on a very fine wind. The guns of Pendennis Castle fired a grand salute as the flotilla sailed by.[8] They would sail first for Bilbao, a seaport in the Province of Biscay, Spain.[9] Francis had been at Falmouth for eleven days, but he had not seen any members of his family. He was within 120 miles of Wolford Lodge, time enough for a coach to cover the distance. However, since his mother and sisters had no word on how long he would be held up, they did not contemplate making the journey.

He posted his first letter from the Peninsula on 13 October, The *Tyne* had dropped anchor at Bilboa after a most miserable voyage. The Spanish people were loud in their welcome to the allies who would help them drive the wicked French from their country. Francis saw lavishly uniformed Spanish officers milling about, and rather scruffily turned out rank and file. He noticed that officers and men alike wore red cockades with "Viva Fernando VII". Early in May, Bonaparte had deposed the popular young monarch and placed his brother Joseph on the throne of Spain, to the outrage of the people. With no French troops near Bilbao the Spanish were free to vent their feelings. Francis watched, proudly as a local band struck up "God Save the King" and "Rule Britannia."[10] The enthusiastic reception Sir David Baird's reinforcements were receiving heartened officers and men who had been cooped up aboard the ships and were keen to land. Francis liked the people immediately and he resolved to learn some Spanish phrases as soon as possible. Sending them home would be certain to amuse Miss Burges.

Francis knew that Baird's force would not be disembarking until the ships reached Corunna, where the Spanish were preparing to accommodate the troops. There, they had promised Baird, wagons for transport, and provisions, would be waiting for them.

Part Four

Lieutenant Francis Simcoe

Chapter 13
Corunna, Lisbon, Cadiz

Nine days after the welcome at Bilboa, Francis was at Corunna, but still living aboard the *Tyne*. He wrote to Elizabeth on 22 October that he expected to be in Sir John Moore's rearguard. Writing again, at ten in the evening of the 24th, he was hoping that the troops would disembark any day. They might march to Biscay to meet Sir John Moore's army. "I hope soon to amuse Miss Burges with some Spanish stories in the Spanish language."

As with his writings in Ireland, Francis was keeping a formal journal, and sending more revealing letters to his mother and sisters. The journal began with the departure from Falmouth:

> We had a very fine wind. We soon got into the Bay of Biscay where our decks were well washed from the sea running very high. We went at the rate of 6 or 7 knots an hour the whole way and after a very satisfactory and favourable passage of 4 days arrived at Corunna harbour on the 13th [October]. It looked very handsome at a distance. We received a salute on entering, it was very curious to see the millions of people that occupied the walks, beach, tops of houses and windows. I supposed that they had never seen such a number of ships together before. We found a two-decker. There were besides frigates. The homes are all tiled; we lay by two large ships full of French prisoners. I was very much pleased with being on firm land on the Continent of Europe.[1]

Although Francis did not know the overall picture, he was aware that Sir David Baird had run into difficulties. Horses were in short supply, and only half the required "batt and forage" money was available. The troops were not receiving orders to disembark, and rations were short.

Sir John Moore's plan was to rendezvous with Sir David Baird's reinforcements near Valladolid. Then, in cooperation with Spanish forces, they would attack the French in November, before winter set in. After marching from Lisbon Moore had reached Salamanca on 13 October. Since Baird had arrived at Corunna the same day, there should have been plenty of time for the reinforcements to march from Corunna and join Moore. Salamanca was only fifty miles from Valladolid.

Spanish half-heartedness, and inefficiency, pride, or plain bad temper, were a bane to Moore and Baird, and in time to Wellesley. The Governor of Corunna refused to allow the British troops to disembark. When the men were finally landed on 26 October, Baird found neither transport wagons nor provisions. Since Baird had little money, he had to borrow from the English plenipotentiary in Spain, Mr. John Hookham Frere. Baird would not be ready to leave Corunna until the end of November.

Francis went ashore with some other officers and visited a coffee house. A major with them understood a little Spanish "so that he was very useful to us". Afterwards they dined and saw a play which was amusing "though I did not understand it." He admired some gypsies, whom he thought very handsome:

> I was much pleased likewise with the fandango dance which I liked very much. The women are small and pretty. The Governor afterwards invited us to come and see the castle, which is uncommonly strong. I was very sorry I had not the opportunity of seeing the inside of it during our stay here.

The Marquess de la Romana arrived and was received joyfully by the people. The inhabitants stopped his state carriage and drew him through the streets. Francis noted that he had arrived in a British frigate. Romana was a distinguished Spanish general whose army had been serving with Napoleon's forces in Denmark. When Spain declared war on France, the Royal Navy had rescued the Marquess and 9,000 of his soldiers, who thus fortuitously became allies. In celebration there were illuminations and fireworks almost every night during Francis' stay at Corunna:

> I was much surprised one day on going ashore for orders to find that an order was issued for the 27th and 31st Regts to prepare themselves for immediate sailing. I was very sorry that we will be departed from this grand army, and on the 25th of October we sailed from Corunna. We left the harbour on a fair wind but it soon changed ... we did not round Cape Finisterre until the 30th and on the 2nd of November we entered the harbour of Lisbon.

The entrance to the Tagus was uncommonly strong and well fortified. In the harbour were several frigates. Sir Henry Burrard, Sir John Moore's superior, was in Lisbon. Francis hoped that the regiment would be able to go with him to join Moore, but the following day they received an order to disembark.[2]

He found quarters at an inconvenient distance from the barracks. He had to pass through several officers' rooms to reach his own, and the billet was

N

PORTUGAL

DUERO

Corunna

Bilbao

Burgos

Valladolid

Oporto

DOURO

Almeida

Celorico

Bussaco

MONDEGO

Gouveia

Guarda

Ciudad Rodrigo

Salamanca

Coimbra

Castelo Branco

Talavera

TAGUS

Madrid

TAGUS

Torres
Vedras

Santarem

Elvas

Badajoz

Olivenza

Albuera

GUADIANA

PORTUGAL

GUADIANA

A

L

I

P

S

Cordova

GUADALQUIVIR

Seville

Malaga

Cadiz

Gibraltar

G. R. D. Fryer

very expensive. He managed to get a small room in another barracks, closer to his men. The weather was very warm, and they were able to have plenty of grapes and melons. He was unhappy that he had no news from England and was feeling lonely.

Sir Charles Colter's fleet lay in the Tagus River, and Francis could see war damage. He did not complain, but he must have been disappointed. The 27th was one of several that had been detached from Sir David Baird's expedition and sent to garrison Lisbon while Baird and Moore were in the field. A strong garrison was indicated because Napoleon himself was in Spain, in command of a combined force of 250,000 French and allied soldiers from several French-occupied countries. He intended to capture Lisbon. Instead, when he found that Moore was across his main line of communication to France, he swung north to destroy him. En route he scattered a Spanish force that was supposed to move to strengthen the British. Baird did not join Moore until 20 December, too late to prevent a retreat to Corunna. Napoleon departed, leaving Marshal Nicolas Soult to pursue Moore.

In Lisbon the men of the 3rd Battalion 27th Regiment were again drilling, keeping up their skills with the musket and bayonet, and endlessly forming squares. Francis was occupied supervising part or all of the company, but also finding time to explore the old city and its magnificent buildings. "Lisbon is a very fine handsome town but very dirty, so much so that you could have no idea of it without seeing it":

I like the Spanish much better than the Portuguese. The latter are great imposors and vagabonds. There is one thing which set me particularly against them, those of them passing by one of our sentinals at night who attacked him and stabbed him so much it rendered him insensible and after all only took away his shoes and stockings and left him in this state. The vagabond could not be found. The man was not expected to live.[3]

Some time in late November or December Great Aunt Margaret died. Francis wrote that he was sorry to hear of the death of Mrs. Graves (he never used a less formal name), although "I believe it is a just relief to herself and my sisters. I am going to send Eliza a very account of my life since I left Middleton collected from my journal." He would not be able to send more letters until ships bringing reinforcements arrived, or "they decide to evacuate Portugal." Jewelry was very cheap in Lisbon, and he would send some home.

Back in London, Lord Moira wrote to Elizabeth Simcoe on 26 November 1808. A lieutenancy in the 27th Regiment was available for purchase. He had taken it upon himself to secure it for Ensign Simcoe. If Mrs. Simcoe approved, he would write to John Ridge Esq., the regimental agent of 44 Charing Cross, and confirm the change. Elizabeth, knowing how thrilled Francis would be, did not hesitate. The commission would cost £550, which meant that she would pay £150, the difference between the price of the lieutenancy and the sale of the ensigncy. The commission was signed on 22 December, a fine belated Christmas gift for Francis.

During the last days of December and into January, Sir John Moore's army was withdrawing to Corunna, where transport ships would rescue the hungry survivors of a dreadful winter march. On 16 January, outside the gates of Corunna the British beat off an attack by Soult, and reached the ships. In the fighting Sir John Moore was killed, and Sir David Baird lost an arm. Napoleon had left the Peninsula, never to return. His marshals would fight the Spanish and British while the emperor was preoccupied with Russia and his occupation of Europe. After the escape of the British from Corunna, Soult turned his army southwards to ravage northern Portugal, and in March he occupied the coastal city of Oporto (Porto) at the mouth of the Douro River.

In February, the 27th and 29th Regiments were dispatched by sea to Cadiz. The commanding officer of the detachment was Major General Alexander Mackenzie who, years before, had been a young Arthur Wellesley's "governor" when he was learning equitation in France. Writing on the 9th Francis explained:

> We came here to garrison this town but do not know whether we shall be allowed to land. There is an officer sent to the Junta at Seville with dispatches which will let us know whether we are to disembark or not. I went ashore yesterday. It is a most beautiful city. The streets are very narrow but uncommonly clean and neat. It is well served, the houses are very pretty and picturesque. The inhabitants did not greet us with as much civility as at Corunna and I am afraid they will not let us land.[4]

The 74th Regiment and four frigates were in the harbour, as well as fourteen or fifteen ships of the line, French and Spanish. The British government impounded the French battleships and put crews aboard to secure them. Cadiz was incredibly strong; a small army could defend it against a very large one. If the troops were not allowed to land, they might go on into the Mediterranean. (The 1st and 2nd Battalions of the 27th Regiment were still located there.)

> I would like to land here very much to garrison the Town. It would be a great opportunity of learning the language. I have lately met with an inconsiderable loss ... we were ordered to leave our baggage behind and to carry nothing more than 3 or 4 shirts and stockings, what we could carry on our backs. I left my trunk on board the baggage ship. It was badly damaged in as much as nobody was left in the ship to take care of it but the master & men and when on sailing from Lisbon we very unluckily, mine & another officer's baggage belonging to this regiment were the only officers who lost it.

He did not know whether he would be granted an allowance, and had to draw £20 of the sum Elizabeth permitted him to tide him over. Francis had not heard of a box Elizabeth had sent to Lisbon, nor did he know "by what conveyance it went." [5]

There had been a "great commotion" in town. The populace were suspicious of the Governor of Cadiz and the Junta in Seville. A mob had murdered a member of the Junta, and thirty people had been put to death. A delegation had gone to General Mackenzie, entreating him to land. Mackenzie was willing, but only if the government asked for the help of the British troops.

Francis had met Colonel and Mrs. Rawdon, and their daughter, relatives of Lord Moira. Miss Rawdon was "very pretty and accomplished." She had been in Italy and was on her way home to England. She was about twenty years old. Through the Rawdons he had met General Richard Stewart, a friend of his father's. The Spanish women were much smaller and more elegant than the Portuguese. "I like their ways very much. [They] are the gentlest people, dress in black silk and beautiful lace." By 3 March he knew they would be returning to Lisbon. "I was uncommonly sorry to see in an English newspaper an account of Escott being burnt down. I hope none of the family have suffered from it and that they are all accounted for." (Escott was the country house of Sir George Yonge, after whom Simcoe had named Toronto's Yonge Street.) He had discovered in another newspaper that his lieutenancy had been signed, before a letter had come from home. "I was happy to hear of my lieutenancy especially as it ensures my staying in the Grenadier Company which perhaps might not have been the case otherwise. I find many comforts derived from it." He signed his letter "F.G. Simcoe, Lieut. of Grenadiers, 3d. Batt. 27th Regt.[6]

The long delays, first at Corunna and now at Cadiz, were very hard on the ordinary soldiers. They had to remain on the troop transports in cramped quarters while Spanish bureaucrats and generals decided whether their honour was intact. Only Officers were permitted to go ashore. Allowing vast numbers of common soldiers access to wine shops could lead to disturbances. The troops had failed to land at Cadiz and were back in Portugal. They had disembarked at Belem, four miles downstream from Lisbon on the 13 March By the 23rd Francis was at Camarate, eight miles north of Lisbon.

It was a small village but here was a floating bridge:

> The only place you can pass, the Tagus being nowhere fordable for 30 or 40 miles, here we are placed to defend this pass as it was thought the French were not many miles off. This is a very beautiful Country but the accomodation [sic] for soldiers is very bad. they were put into any old houses rather barns, that they could find I was in a small unfurnished house with nothing to depend upon but my blanket. There was adjoining it however a most beautiful garden & the largest orange grove I ever beheld

as well as lemons... .There is one thing I passed over [in his last letter] which I saw in Lisbon namely the aquaduct, it is the grandest thing I ever saw, it runs for a length of 25 miles & conveys water into Lisbon by pipes over hill & vale; I was in a valley over which it runs & the arches were so uncommonly high that it exceeds any idea you could form of it.[7]

The Aquaduct at Lisbon which Francis Simcoe described in a letter to his mother.

The troops were all in quarters and exercising after the long confinement at Cadiz. Francis had heard of the Duke of York's disgrace, and wondered who would succeed him. The Duke had done no wrong, but his mistress had been taking bribes in return for influencing His Royal Highness to grant promotions. After reading some of Captain John Simcoe's manuscripts, Francis commented, "He must have been a very clever man and perfectly Master of his profession." The French were on the move, advancing towards the borders of Portugal in three columns of 15,000 men each.[8]

Spring of 1809 had brought many developments of importance. Not the least was the appointment of Sir Arthur Wellesley, cleared of blame for the Cintra Convention, as commander in chief in the Peninsula. Sir Hew Dalrymple had been long gone. Now Sir John Cradock, commander in chief and senior to Wellesley, had been ordered to take command of the garrison at Gibraltar. Francis did not approve; he felt that Cradock had been badly treated. He sent his sisters a copy of Sir John's message to the troops at Lisbon, in which he praised them for the the good conduct of officers and men during a trying period.[9]

The British force gathered at Camarate was 9,000 strong, and they await-ed only the arrival of General Rowland Hill, with 6,000 more to bring it to 15,000. In addition, 3,000 Portuguese were ready to take to the field. The Por-tuguese authorities had responded more positively than the Spanish to the British presence. The Spanish troops, under Spanish officers, were badly trained but the Junta would not allow British officers to interfere. The Por-tuguese willingly allowed Major General William Carr Beresford to train their army. Beresford was not a brilliant field commander, but he had the skill to prepare men for action. He was fluent in the Portuguese language because he had served in Madeira. Throughout the past few months, Beresford had worked wonders with the Portuguese army.

For Lieutenant Francis Simcoe, the pace was quickening. Wellesley was back, preparing to take the army against Oporto. They would soon march along the Tagus, then north for "a real fight":

> I think should we meet the French, ... and they are not more than [their present strength] we shall do their business for them especially as our troops are in high health and spirits and quite fresh while on the other hand the French labour under all the disadvantages of long marches through the enemy's country. The wild flowers here are beautiful and curious.

"The paper on which the last letter was wrote is the best this country affords, but I got this from the paymaster." (This may be why some letters he wrote in March are very faint.) No letters were waiting for him when he returned to Lisbon, likely because they had been forwarded to Cadiz.[10]

To "Dearest Sisters" Francis regretted not being able to write to them often, but their mother would pass on all the news:

> I write you a few lines to [tell you] how much I love and think of you as it is thought likely that we may not be long before we see the enemy... I like very much to have you here for a few weeks to shew you a most beautiful country. The climate is also very fine, but all the country hous-es are forsaken. There is not a gentleman to be seen in them and it is a great pity to see all the Orchards lemon and orange groves going to ruin for want of cultivation... on many parts of the road between here and Lisbon there are small images stuck up which [men] never think of pass-ing without taking off their hats and making a low bow.[11]

At last, on 8 April, the brigades gathered at Camarate were ready to advance. General Hill had arrived with the 6,000 men, his own and several other brigades. Francis enclosed a plan of the line of brigades, surely a serious breach of security. If the ship carrying it was captured it would fall into the wrong hands.

The plan showed the commander in chief as Sir Arthur Wellesley, successor to Sir John Cradock; the second in command was Sir Edward Paget, succeeding General John Sherbrooke. On the plan the battalion number was given first, the regiment second.

In our leaving Camarate we were being added as from:
1st Brigade 2/48, 2/66, 5/60 Maj. Gen. [Rowland] Hill
2nd Brigade 3/27, 2/31, 1/45 Maj. Gen. [Alexander]McKenzie [sic]
3rd Brigade 3/Buffs, 2/87, 3/27, 2/88 Maj. Gen. [Christopher] Tilson
4th Brigade 2/detachments, 97th, Maj. Gen. [Samuel] Sankey
5th Brigade 2/Royal Fusiliers, 2/53 F., Brig. Gen. [?]
6th Brigade 1/detachments, 29th F., Brig. Gen. [?]
7th Brigade 2/30, 2/83, Brig. Gen. [John] Cameron Brigade of Cavalry 14 Lt. Dragoons, 18 do. & do., 3rd K. G. [King's German] Legion, 4 Portuguese Cavalry, Gen.[Sir Stapleton] Cotton.

The men of the 5th Battalion, 60th Regiment were armed with rifles, an innovation. Riflemen were better suited to skirmishing than those armed with muskets that were faster to load but of shorter range and less accurate. "Detachments" refer to battalions put together from remnants of other units.

Since the list had been made, more cavalry had been brigaded, and more infantry regiments were on the way. Major General Paget had landed and would command a division when more troops had joined the army from England. Such a large army had to be moved in stages, some battalions or wings using different roads.

The seven brigades marched up the north bank of the Tagus, passing through many small villages some of whose names are not on modern maps. Accommodation varied from a sumptuous home that had belonged to "The Patriarch" to collections of small rooms that offered cramped space for all the officers. The left wing halted at Villa Verde (many places had this name). The right wing, with the Grenadier Company, marched a mile further towards the top of a very high mountain to a large convent. The walks and gardens about the buildings were very beautiful.

The descent from the mountains was impressive. They passed a pretty town that seemed to have been a fortress. The walls were very high and thick, and Francis thought one ruin might be the remains of what had been a citadel. Because of hot baths, the place was esteemed for curing familiar diseases. At one village the officers stayed in a very large monastery, where the monks treated them handsomely. More than 150 officers dined and breakfasted with them. Francis thought it could easily contain 10,000 troops. The kitchen was enormous, "with every sort of convenience and luxury to be found. At one end was a large fountain and an immense quantity of fish, fowl and meat would have almost supplied a whole army. "The country we passed over was very fine. In some places we were not a league from the sea."

(A league, he explained to Elizabeth, was four English miles).

They left Batalha on 23 April and stopped at Leira. At that point twelve regiments were travelling together, as well as artillery and cavalry. Here Sir John Cradock departed, handing over his command, although Sir Arthur Wellesley had not yet arrived from Lisbon "He [Wellesley] was received with great enthusiasm by the inhabitants of Lisbon and every town he passed through."

> We marched to Ourem about 5 leagues. I observed that we were going more to the right than we otherwise should had we been going to Oporto which it was supposed we were, and on arriving at Ourem we were told that we were marching off towards the Tagus, and the main army, our brigade excepted, 3rd Batt 27, 2nd Batt 31, 1st Batt 45 comprised fine regiments with our Brigade of artillery gone to Oporto. Here was the second time that our regiment has had the misfortune to be detached from the main army.

> For my part I am very sorry for I would sooner be commanded by Sir Arthur Wellesley than any other General that is in army. We are now to fight with the Portuguese troops who I fear will not be much good.

They halted at Abrantes, where Francis wrote a long account of events:

> We are to attack who is on the other side of the Tagus if we can collect sufficient force, otherwise to defend the Tagus and not allow them to pass it.[12]

Thus while Wellesley and most of the army were nearing Oporto to attack Soult, the 27th Regiment would be among those placed to prevent Marshal Claude Victor-Perrin from effecting a junction with Soult. On 29 March, Marshal Victor had already done Wellesley considerable damage, by routing at Medellin a Spanish army led by General Gregorio Cuesta that had been marching to support the British. To everyone's regret, the men of Francis' brigade were also losing Major General Mackenzie, who would remain with Wellesley's brigades.

Chapter 14
First March to Badajoz

On 9 May General Mackenzie said farewell to his brigade. He requested Colonel John Maclean to tell the officers and men of the 27th Regiment how much he appreciated their services. Earlier, Francis wrote to Elizabeth, General Mackenzie had told the "commander of forces" (then Sir John Cradock) of the regiment's good behaviour, especially an occasion when they marched for thirty miles through a difficult and mountainous country where the battalion was forced to go in single file, and succeeded in not leaving a single man behind:

> Genl McKenzie cannot allow the 27th Regt to march without expressing his sincere regret at the separation, and thanking the officers and men for their uniform regular and soldierlike conduct during the whole of the time they were under his command. This reflects more credit on the attention of the officers and disposition of the men as the Battn was formed of very young materials but a short time before they were sent on service.

From Ourem the brigade marched to Tomar, where the 31st Regiment remained. A great many Portuguese troops were in the area. "The Grenadier Company escorted the guns to a large farm house about half a league beyond Peneta, a small town. The house was indeed commodious. The gardens and groves were well supplied. The outhouses were very considerable and had a cellar full of wine about 100 yards in length. The man who appeared to own it sold everything at an immense price and then told his master that the soldiers broke in and took everything away. They moved on to Abrantes, and arrived on 5 May:

> [Here] we are likely to stay some time although we have received an order to hold ourselves in readiness to march at an hour's notice and always to have three days provisions ready cooked. The 4th Dragoons are coming here today and there are more troops expected.

On 12 May Wellington took Oporto from Soult. The French marshal had ordered all boats along the Douro collected and bridges blocked. Wellington's men found some wine boats discreetly hidden along the south side of the river, and were able to effect a crossing. General Beresford's troops stayed along the Tagus from Abrantes to the Spanish border until 11 June, but Marshal Victor's force did not appear. "We have about 5,000 Portuguese troops and Marshal [sic] Beresford is gone with about the same number. Gen. [Francisco] Miranda is left with what fatigued troops are here but they are wretchedly bad."[1]

Miranda was a Venezuelan, and a rebel against Spanish rule, but now he was serving the mother country. Early in 1808, he had hoped that Britain would send Wellesley in command of the troops gathered in Ireland to assist an insurrection against Spain. Instead they had been sent to Portugal. Miranda was one more useless general. Francis' opinion of the Portuguese was rising as his esteem for the Spanish crumbled.

On 22 May, Francis told Elizabeth that he had just heard of the defeat of Marshal Soult. Marshal Victor had fallen back on his main army and crossed a bridge at Murcello which Mr. Robert Wilson's Lusitania Legion had defended bravely. The "Marquis Cuesta" with 22,000 Spanish troops was supposed to be in the rear of Marshal Victor. He cast light on the composition of Wellesley's force by the summer of 1809. Both the British and French armies had troops from allied or conquered countries. Exiles from French-occupied Hanover served in the infantry and cavalry of the King's German Legion. As well as a Lusitanian Legion, Wellesley counted among his troops *Chasseurs Britanniques*, French emigrés who had left France during the revolution and the unsettled times of the 1790s. Francis still thought he would see action very soon:

> although we have had the misfortune of not being present at the defeat of
> Marshal Soult we may yet hope to defeat Marshal Victor. It would be a
> great disappointment to me to have been present in Portugal at the hour
> of the defeat of the French and yet not see a shot fired. Sir A. Wellesley is
> coming over this way as fast as possible.

He closed with, "That God Almighty may ever bless and protect my dear Mother is ever the wish of her affect. Son F.G. Simcoe. Remember me affect to my Brother and Sisters. Then he added a postscript. "I have met with an old schoolfellow of mine in the 4th Dragoons. There is another in the 3rd, indeed there is hardly a regiment in which I do not meet with an Etonian.[2]

Following his defeat at Oporto, Marshal Soult was withdrawing his army back into Spain, by way of Almeida, Ciudad Rodrigo and from there south towards Marshal Victor's troops. Wellesley was retracing his steps southwards as far as Abarantes. Francis fully expected Beresford's brigades to join Wellesley, but an order arrived for the 27th Regiment, among others, to withdraw to Lisbon. Francis was decidedly upset:

FRANCIS SIMCOE, 27TH REGT

Peter W. Johnson '91

Artist's conception, a grenadier officer of the 27th (Inniskilling) Regiment. Except for his coat, his uniform is a mixture of parade and campaign dress. Grenadiers wore bearskin caps on parade, but they substituted shakos in the field. Soldiers in Wellington's army wore whatever was serviceable.

We have just received an addition of 255 men to our battalion which makes us 1055 strong. Can they leave such a battalion in garrison and keep regiments 500 strong and not better men, even for political reasons. There are seven regiments encamped here. I cannot say much for their appearance compared to the fine troops Sir Arthur Wellesley has with him.[3]

While the 27th and the other regiments were marching southwest along the Tagus, Wellesley led the victors of Oporto from Abrantes in the opposite direction, into Spain. The men of the 27th had been told that boats would meet them, but they found none and continued their march. Francis passed through Santarem, the largest town after Abrantes, in a rainstorm. At a small town downstream some boats were waiting, enough for the men unfit to march, and Colonel Maclean placed Francis in charge of them. "This place I left this morning [17 June] with the sick of the Regiments and went by water to Lisbon where I arrived at 11 o'clock in the morning." All along the route the countryside was a perfect garden, so much more lush than on the march north in April.

At Lisbon he noticed that the ships in the harbour were different. He recognized the *Barfleur*, the flagship of Admiral George Cranfield Berkeley, a long-standing family friend. The Admiral soon invited Francis to breakfast aboard, the very thing any lad with the prodigious appetite of a seventeen-year-old valued most:

The civility of the Berkeley family was very great... The Bishop of Oporto, a man of advanced years and who for his gallant conduct in that city has since been made patriarch, and the British Ambassador, several of the Regency* &c came on board about 11 o'clock. The yards of all the men of war were manned. We went through the cabins &c and into the Admiral's where a most elegant and sumptuous breakfast was prepared after which we went completely through the ship and after every wing being seen went to the different ships the grand and most beautiful sights I had ever seen.[4]

*The Portuguese Prince Regent and the old Queen, had travelled in British vessel to Brazil in 1807, leaving some staff in Lisbon to look out for their interests.

Admiral Berkeley hosted a dance every Thursday, to which Francis had a standing invitation. By August he was worried over Elizabeth's *very very* long silence, and wondering if some accident had befallen her. He begged her to reply without delay. His letters were being forwarded by Admiral Berkeley on a vessel he was about to send home. Many times when he did not hear from home over long periods, Francis suspected letters of being lost at sea.

By the time he was writing, he had heard what had happened when Wellesley and the Spanish General Cuesta clashed with Napoleon's Marshals Victor and Sebastiani on 27-28 July. The place was Talavera, on the bank of the Tagus seventy miles southwest of Madrid. Sir Arthur had some 20,000 British troops, and Cuesta 33,000 Spaniards. Victor and Sebastiani had 50,000. After a bad beginning during which two of his battalions were mauled by the French, Wellesley concentrated on arming the Medellin Hill. In front lay a plain, bisected by the Portina Stream. Spain has a climate called "Mediterranean", meaning winter rain and summer drought. The plain was now parched, the grass dried greyish yellow.

Plagued by untrained troops who fired their muskets before the French were within range, broke and fled, Cuesta's force did not bear the weight of the French attack. What amounted to Wellesley's own 20,000 soldiers were placed on and around Medillon Hill, the kind of position Sir Arthur liked. The French would have to attack his position, not he theirs. When they did, losses on both sides were horrendous, but the defeated Victor withdrew. Wellesley and Cuesta lost 6,200 killed and wounded to Victor's 7,390. Tragically, a fire ignited the dry grass, and many wounded on both sides perished before they could be rescued. Spain had let down the British, not only for Cuesta's dismal performance, but by failing to send provisions as promised. Before the battle began Wellesley's troops were on half rations, or less. When he withdrew, Wellesley left 1,500 wounded men. The Spanish promised to care from then, but again their pledge was worthless. When the French reoccupied Talavera they treated the British with the same care they gave their own wounded.

"The glorious battle of Talavera you must have had a full account of, which, with its hero [Wellesley] will ever hold an high name in the annals of history." Francis could write thus because he was not there. He had not yet witnessed the true horror of a bloodbath. In the next breath he found reality. Major General Alexander Mackenzie, whom he held in highest esteem, fell at Talavera. "The loss of our most excellent and beloved officer, Maj. Genl McKenzie will never be forgotten." Farther on he wrote:

I think France cannot hold Spain. I am quite disgusted at the Spaniards. Their many uncivilities to our officers, their supplying our troops badly and one thing and another make them appear to me jealous & disaffected.[5]

Wellesley had been able to defeat superior numbers because of the positions he chose, and the different fighting styles of the British and Napoleonic armies. British musketmen stood in two ranks facing the enemy advance, firing by platoons. The British practiced with live ammunition, and none of the European armies Napoleon's army defeated were as well trained.

The French attacked in solid columns, so that only the front and part of the side ranks could fire their muskets without hitting some of their own. By not presenting a wider front they allowed the highly trained British infantrymen to destroy the exposed French ranks. A few from within the column might fire as those in front fell, but with a shambles developing in front of them the men behind might break and run. Napoleon scorned the use of rifles, because they were slower to reload.

A musket was accurate for only fifty yards, a rifle four times that length. The men of the 60th Regiment could start skirmishing many yards before the French muskets could strike them. Skirmishing by riflemen supported by light company muskets was more effective than that by musketmen alone. When the time came, Francis' Grenadiers would stand in the two-line formations, as steady as on a parade ground, determinedly firing and reloading, keeping their dressing by closing up where a comrade dropped. Then, when the attack had been blunted, fixing bayonets and charging, adding their extra weight to wherever the line threatened to break.

Immediately after his success at Talavera, Wellesley withdrew his army back into Portugal to avoid a confrontation with Soult, who was moving to join Victor. He could not afford to be cut off in Spain, particularly with his men half starved owing to Spanish broken promises. In Portugal his army could always be supplied by the Royal Navy, an advantage Napoleon's marshals did not have. The land route back to France was narrow, the roads poor, and the British naval squadrons blocked the sea lanes. French troops lived off the country, stripping it bare, to the fury of the Spanish landed gentry and peasant farmers. Wellesley's orders were for his army to pay for anything they had to take from the local people, and to depend on their own rations as much as possible.

Wellesley had already begun to reorganize his army into a new formation, the division, consisting of two or more brigades, each supported by one company of riflemen, and usually two squadrons of cavalry. The 27th Regiment was placed in the 4th Division, commanded by Major General Sir Galbraith Lowry Cole.

Known as Lowry, rather than Galbraith, Cole had long standing ties with the 27th Regiment. He was the Dublin-born second son of the 1st Earl of Enniskillen, and a former commander of the 2nd Battalion 27th Foot. He had been second-in-command at the Battle of Maida in July 1806, after which the regiment was allowed to count Maida among its battle honours. He was assigned to Wellesley's 4th Division, initially of two English brigades. One brigade was of the 7th and 23rd, both fusiliers. Francis remembered that his grandfather, Thomas Gwillim, had once served in the 7th Fusiliers. A fusil was a musket, but shorter and lighter than the muskets issued to other line regiments. In Francis' brigade were his own battalion, the 40th and 48th. General John Harvey's Portuguese Brigade would follow them. The 4th Division, with the 3rd and Light Divisions, were reputed to contain Wellesley's best brigades. Now that Major General Mackenzie was dead, the command of Francis' brigade went to Colonel James Kemmis, commander of the 40th Regiment. Little is known about Kemmis beyond his name on the Army List, and a remark by Francis that he was "generally very much disliked".[6]

In September Sir Arthur Wellesley was created Viscount Wellington of Talavera. He could not be Lord Wellesley because his eldest brother, Richard, already had that title. His elder brother William arbitrarily chose Wellington after a town in the county of Somerset. Arthur approved, but his wife Kitty did not because it had no significance for the family. At that time, Richard Lord Wellesley had been appointed the British Ambassador to the Junta in Cadiz. Richard persuaded Arthur, whom Francis now had to think of as Lord Wellington, to station his army at Badajoz for two or three months. British troops encamped there would hearten the Spanish garrison and assure them of continued British support. The withdrawal back to Portugal had unnerved the Junta members. Wellington ordered Kemmis' Brigade to march to Badajoz because they were fresh troops. The rest of his army was exhausted.

Two pairs of great fortresses guarded the valleys of the Douro and Guardiana Rivers, two accessible points along the Portuguese-Spanish frontier. On the Portuguese side were Almeida in the north, and Elvas in the south. The Spanish guardians were Ciudad Rodrigo in the north and Badajoz (the strongest of all) in the south. In the autumn of 1809 the French had not captured any of them. (By the spring of 1811 only Elvas would be in allied hands.)

That autumn of 1809, at Badajoz, the troops would go into into a "cantonment", for a rest, although Francis knew his men did not need it. Wellington needed the garrison from Lisbon as a reinforcement because so many Talavera veterans were ill or recovering from wounds, exertions and malnutrition. Cantonments were more substantial than encampments set up during marches or for short stays. Where possible, officers received billets, and the men were "hutted", rather than in tents. Bivouacking in shelters of boughs or of thatch made on the spot was usual on a march where tents, for the men in the ranks as well as the officers, would have been too cumbersome.

According to Francis' journal, the regiment left Lisbon on 28 September 1809. Boats ferried them across the Tagus, where it was several miles wide, and stopped at Aldea Galega, a small scattered village that commanded a fine view of Lisbon. Here the men bivouacked. For the night of the 29th, they stopped five leagues on (twenty miles) at Pegos Velhos, where they found just one house for the officers. The men lay down in a wood for the night:

> We either marched at one or two o'clock in the morning during the whole of the march to Badajoz. I was left with a party of 15 Grenadiers to accompany some cars [carts] [along] another road, after which I was to make the rest of my way to the Regiment. Although I did not march til daylight, we were under arms at one o'clock. About 12 o'clock in the day I left the cars at their destination and proceeded to join the regiment and

other strangers in the country. You may suppose I knew nothing of the day, however I had a map of guards from a corps receiving His Majety's pay to direct me the way, but somehow or other in the night he lost his road 4 o'clock at night we found from information from a lonely house that we were 8 leagues from Aldea Galega.[7]

They marched another league and lay down to rest on a barren heath "being unable to continue, after marching through a difficult country." After more enquiries, he found that they were not four leagues from Vendas Novas, where they arrived at eleven o'clock at night "almost knocked up." Marching on they came to Montemor-o-Novo. Here they found "a curious old castle on an high emminence" he thought must be Moorish. It commanded an extensive view." On 4 October they reached the walled town of Arraiolos and ramparts "but little calculated for the present method of wafare." Heavy guns would make short work of the masonry. On the 5th they were at Estremoz. The country around was beautiful, covered with vinyards and the grapes "in the highest perfection."

By 6 October they arrived at a wood a little beyond Elvas, where they lay for the night:

> The reason for our not pressing to Elvas was there being the sick and wounded of the army in that city. I had not much time, but I just went in to take a glimpse of the town, and did not care to be very long, … I understand there is only one part accessible, it is a large and very good town. I would like to have spent a few days there as it would take three or four days to study the outworks.[8]

On the 8th they left the wood near Elvas and entered Badajoz:

> It is a most beautiful town and you have a fine view of both cities the most part of the way. The bridge across the Guardiana [River] into Badajoz is very magnificent. Badajoz is about the same size as Elvas and cleaner, but proves to [hold] near double the force.[9]

"I know no more about politics than the man in the moon," he continued. But he knew something had to be done about false rumours and reports in the papers about "our army." All the officers were not tired of war. "However a few underestimate who are tired of the business and would much rather be in Bond Street" but that did not apply to the whole army. He knew many officers who thought exactly as he did:

> I never was (Thank God) in better health & spirits although I find there is a vast deal of differences between the Portuguese and the Spanish I do not wholly understand or do not find the Spanish here as civil as the Portuguese and they are not very partial to each other.[10]

He was sending a few "trifles" home as he expected very soon to be on active service. He hoped a topaz ring with a very fine stone would be acceptable. He had bought it in Lisbon to remind him of the city. Three bottles of perfume he bought in Cadiz were from Tangier, and very cheap. "You will [know] how best to dispose of them. The stopper had come out of one of the bottles by some accident and the best part was lost. "If you think it handsome enough, suppose you were to make a present of one of the bottles to Julia" (a full one, of course).

Other items might be for Sophia and Caroline. The handkerchief was for Katherine. "The names and places are not very very clear, but I daresay it will amuse her particularly as I bought it in Badajoz on purpose for her." Then he had an after thought. The Topaz truly was a lovely stone:

> If you think Julia would like the ring I will find something that shall please you just as well, but my reason for not mentioning it first was that it was not so well set as it might be and I thought young Ladies were very particular about the setting.[11]

He was closing the letter because the hour was late and he had to be up by first light to prepare for an inspection by Colonel Kemmis (the very much disliked officer). On 9 October he wrote with relief that the inspection had been cancelled owing to very heavy rain. He was much obliged to Charlotte for a very long and pleasant letter he received from her as soon as he arrived in Badajoz. She had given him all the Devon news, and was an excellent corresondent. He was sending a packet with George Humphrey, his first captain in the 27th Regiment, who would be going to England on leave and would carry it with him. Entrusting valuables to a fellow officer was much more reliable than the post, and it cost less.

He probably gave his family more information than they could absorb, but he left out one detail that embarrassed him. Wellington had prohibited all stealing from the Spanish people. Men from the 27th had robbed bee hives, and the other troops had nicknamed them the "honeysuckers."[12]

On 19 November, still in cantonment at Badajoz, Francis was happy to have such an interesting letter from Elizabeth, dated 5 October from Carnarvon, Wales. As she had requested, he was sending his reply to Stowe, the home of the George Grenville 1st Marquis of Buckingham, where she would be making a lengthy visit. He was glad she had enjoyed her tour of Wales (her favourite place to visit). Francis was wearied of being at Badajoz, and no one seemed to know how much longer they would be kept resting in the cantonment. Many boats had come up the Guardiana from the Gulf of Cadiz, and many carriages had arrived. As he had heard of peace between Austria and France, he did not know how the British army could possibly stay in the Penin-

sula when Napoleon would be in a position to send more troops. Lord Wellington had been in Seville and had returned after seeing his brother Richard
embark at Cadiz for England:

> The army is I am sorry to say very sickly at present, our regiment is the
> healthiest I believe in the army. We have not above 30 sick, which is very
> few from a regiment 800 strong which is the strength of our regiment
> now. Are you acquainted with a Coll of the 14th Lt. Dragoons who is
> here.He is a brother of the Talbot you know in America.[13] (By that time
> Thomas Talbot, aide de camp to Simcoe, had returned after several
> years in Britain to found his own little empire, the Talbot Settlement,
> in southwestern Upper Canada.)

The countryside was now very barren. the only thing worth seeing was a
hill which commanded a fine view of Badajoz, Elvas, and Campo Maior,
towns where British troops were quartered. All the officers thereabout were
billeted with the meanest people in the town. "No nobleman or man of fortune
will allow any officer to be billeted on them" and the Junta "are too much
infatuated to enforce it and which is more, a Briton is not allowed to walk on
the ramparts":

> The countryside around Badajoz abounds with hares and indeed with a
> gun you might have a very good sport. I was very near picking up the
> other day with a double nosed Spanish pointer which I should have liked
> to bring home as they are such excellent dogs and remarkable for being
> very faithful.[14]

By the beginning of December the army was packing up and starting out
for Lisbon. The 4th Division would be the last to leave. Lord Wellington, who
had been away in Lisbon for some weeks, was back at his headquarters, a large
house in Badajoz. Returning to his own poor lodgings, Francis was startled to
find a note from one of Wellington's secretaries. His Lordship was requesting
the pleasure of Lieutenant Simcoe's company at dinner the following afternoon.[15]

Chapter 15

1810 First Battle: Bussaco

Francis stared hard at the invitation from the commander in chief. The Simcoe family did not count the Wellesleys among their friends. Thus far, high-ranking officers had been kind to him out of respect for his father. He decided that someone, most likely John Pring, had told His Lordship that this junior lieutenant was the son of a lieutenant general, Wellington's present rank. To his great satisfaction he discovered he was mistaken.

When he informed Colonel Maclean of the invitation, as he felt dutybound to do, his battalion commander smiled knowingly. Wellington may have known who Francis' father was, but that would not have mattered. The general made a point of having junior officers to dine with him regardless of family connections. He enjoyed the company of the younger men, and he especially sought out those who were showing promise. He wanted the opportunity to form his own opinion of them. Maclean admitted that the reports James Kemmis sent to headquarters had singled Francis out as the brightest hope among his subalterns. Now that he was in command of a brigade, Kemmis had been promoted brigadier general. Francis never hinted whether he had grown fonder of Kemmis. Always at the back of his consciousness was his grandfather's maxim that he who could not obey could never command, and he intended to command.

He ordered his servant to unpack his dress uniform and to brush it well. It was somewhat faded but in better condition than his everyday coat. He eyed the black leather shako with a frown. For field duty the officers and men of the Grenadiers wore shakos similar to those issued to the enlisted men of the battalion companies. He had been wearing his shako when he served as the baggage guard, and the handsome bearskin cap had vanished when his trunk was damaged. The time for the dinner was three o'clock in the afternoon, not one, his usual time. He resolved on a snack to tide himself over.

He felt he looked his best, his gold buttons shiny, breeches very white, boots highly polished, when he arrived at the door to headquarters. He was ushered into a large room where several other young men were waiting, making small talk. All fell silent at the sound of boots tapping on the marble floor of the hallway. The general entered, flanked by two staff officers. This was the first time Francis had seen him close up. Wellington wore a plain dark blue coat, white breeches above shining boots. His dark hair was wavy at the sides of his thin face. Most impressive were his sharp, penetrating eyes and the hooked nose. No wonder the men had nicknamed their hero "Nosey."

Francis was delighted at how quickly the general's greeting put the guests at their ease. At first talk was general, but then it switched to the more specific matters on which they wanted their chief's opinions. Hesitant initially, some voiced their distaste for the Spanish. At that Wellington gave his famous laugh, which brother officers had declared was a war whoop. Francis, who recalled true whoops, thought it more like the fog horn he could hear from the family summer house at Budleigh Salterton. Wellington waxed forth on the Spaniards who were invaluable. True, the Junta and the army were a lodestone around his neck, but without partisans the losses suffered by the British army would have been far heavier. The common people, especially rural peasants, hated the Junta and the military for their poor showing. They formed small bands to harass the French. Among them were his best sources of French intentions. They supplied information, and Wellington supported them with payments and equipment. All this was in confidence, he warned them, but Francis suspected that many already knew.

Writing to Elizabeth on 11 December, Francis dealt briefly with the honour bestowed on him by the commander in chief. "I dined with Ld Wellington a few days back. He keeps a very elegant table and is very pleasant & agreeable."[1]

By that time the 4th Division was nearly packed and ready to depart from Badajoz. Their ultimate objective, they had been told, was Lisbon, but their route turned out to be circuitous. Francis' spelling of place names was phonetic and misleading, but the map he drew later when he had access to more than oral information, clarified the picture. They marched from Badajoz into Portugal, then swung north and reached Portalegre on 28 December. They turned west to Abrantes, Tomar, and Leira. The Portuguese troops he saw at Leira he found "wonderfully improved." He looked forward to seeing how steady they would be under fire. He had no doubts that his Grenadiers would be otherwise than calm and firm. They marched north to Coimbra, where they arrived on 10 January 1810.

On the way he encountered snow for the first time in Portugal, and he remembered wearing warm fur-lined moccasins that would have been so much more serviceable than boots. He recalled the squeak of the snows in sub-zero weather of the Canadian woods. Portuguese snow was slushy and soaked in between his toes.

Coimbra, he noted, was a university town. He may not have remembered that his father had been there. Simcoe had written Eliza from Coimbra in 1806, where he had been taken to recover from the effects of the paint on the ship *Illustrious*. They finally halted at Gouveia. On 16 January he wrote Elizabeth

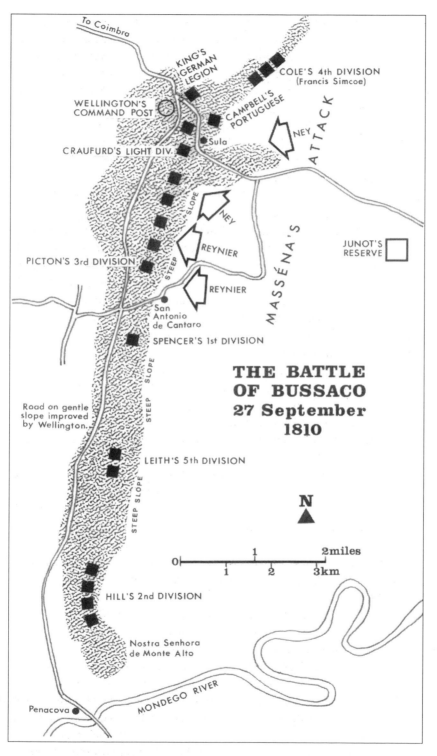

To Coimbra

KING'S
GERMAN
LEGION

COLE'S 4th DIVISION
(Francis Simcoe)

WELLINGTON'S
COMMAND POST

CAMPBELL'S
PORTUGUESE

Sula

NEY ATTACK

CRAUFURD'S LIGHT DIV.

NEY

SLOPE

REYNIER

MASSÉNA'S

JUNOT'S
RESERVE

PICTON'S 3rd DIVISION

STEEP

REYNIER

San
Antonio
de Cantaro

SPENCER'S 1st DIVISION

THE BATTLE
OF BUSSACO
27 September
1810

STEEP SLOPE

Road on gentle
slope improved
by Wellington.

N

LEITH'S 5th DIVISION

STEEP SLOPE

0   1   2miles

1   2   3km

HILL'S 2nd DIVISION

Nostra Senhora
de Monte Alto

MONDEGO RIVER

Penacova

G. R. D. Fryer

that they were in camp after being on a long march for three weeks through mountainous country. He was happy to be back among the Portuguese after the cavalier treatment the Spaniards had meted out. "The change of manners & temper of the inhabitants" was gratifying. Wellington was then at Viseu, across the Mondego River, about forty miles from Gouveia where the regiment was encamped. Francis was confused over the route they were ordered to follow. "We are to hold ourselves in readiness to march on the shortest notice... where we are going God knows, but they are supplying us in order that we may be ready to take the field immediately."[2]

The march of the 4th Division did not make much sense to Francis and the other junior officers. Perhaps the only man who knew what they were about was the divisional commander, Major General Lowry Cole. Wellington's headquarters and his troop movements were a smoke screen to cover the real work of the winter. During his weeks of absence, officially in Lisbon while his army rested at Badajoz, Wellington had been riding with his chief officer of the Royal Engineers, Colonel Richard Fletcher. They had studied the terrain around Torres Vedras, farther up the peninsula that extended north of Lisbon between the Tagus River and the sea.

By December most of his army, British and Portuguese and the other nationalities, were divided into working parties. Wellington had hired thousands of Portuguese labourers to help the soldiers build a line of fortifications outside Lisbon that he prayed the French would not be able to break apart no matter how heavy their guns, nor how clever their miners. Thus far, unlike the French, Wellington's army had few miners or sappers. He had recommended the formation of a corps of sappers and miners, men skilled in construction and the use of explosives, to work under officers of the Royal Engineers, but so far Horse Guards told him to use his troops for digging fortifications and trenches.

Wellington was having three lines of fortifications built. The outermost, twenty-nine miles long, extended from the coast to the Tagus at Alhandra. He expected that it would hold up the French while his troops fell back before the much stronger second line. Twenty-two miles long, it was being built six miles south of the first. This one combined artillery batteries, trenches, redoubts, stockades and ditches. The third line was near the entrance to the Tagus. If all else failed this line would delay the French until Wellington could embark his army. The French would not be able to get round the ends of the innermost line because they would be guarded by Admiral Berkeley's gunboats and frigates. Finally Francis became aware that something of the kind was happening:

Lord Wellington [is] determined upon defending Portugal if England will supply us with troops and my opinion is from the strong position ...that with 25,000 troops which is the number [outside Lisbon] he had engaged to defend it, which he may against treble the number ...the

Spaniards even while determined to resist the French yoke though not so warm in others cause as they might be. I think we shall come to blows ere long. We have not had a sick man since we left Babajoz, we are now without a doubt the strongest regiment in the army.[3]

The University at Coimbra which Francis visited.

In closing he sent his love to his sisters and Henry. "I must not forget to thank Katherine for her interesting & worth while letters which ... gave me a great deal of pleasure." Francis' next letter is dated 16 March, from Guarda, in very high rocky country. The British army was gathering around the upper reaches of the Mondego River and preparing to confront Marshal André. Masséna. Francis had been at Celorico, now Wellington's headquarters, on the 14th. In the interval between the end of January and early March he may have been ill and sent to Lisbon to recover.[4]

On 6 July he wrote from Celorico, now the Head Quarters of the British Army. He had arrived the day before, and would proceed to his regiment which was at Guarda, three leagues distant. He had come by sea from Lisbon to Oporto, where he had left most of his baggage. He would have to send for it and hope it would not be lost, because he would be in the neighbourhood of Guarda for some time. The French had invested Almeida, forty miles away from Guarda, with a strong force of 12,000 men. Wellington had massed his army close enough to be able to control a French advance further into Portugal should Almeida fall. The enemy were also investing

The Portuguese Tradw and Tourism Commission, Toronto.

Ciudad Rodrigo, which fell on the 10th, only four days after Francis wrote his letter. He was soon ill again. On 20 July he wrote from Lisbon:

> You will be much surprised at seeing my letter dated Lisbon, but in consequence of a second fever which attacked me and which was succeeded by a dreadful swelling of my legs & thighs I was ordered to attend a

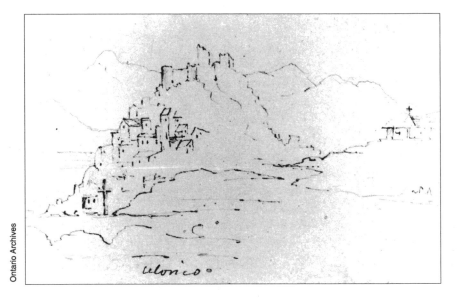

> medical board appointed to report on the state of my health. I immediately left Guarda for Lisbon which I reached in twelve days, a distance of above 200 miles. On my leaving Guarda my mule had a sore back which obliged me to part with him for little or nothing. I had then to purchase a horse for myself to ride and a mule for my baggage on my account here.

He resolved to remain in Lisbon a week, and if he was not improving he would come home because he had accumulated three months' leave. Now, however, he was feeling better and would return to the army shortly:

> I told Dr. Bolton who attends me & is the first medical man in this country, that without it was absolutely necessary I should not wish to leave the country at the present moment. He agrees with me in every point and says that in a few days he hopes to see me as well as ever I was in my life.

> I have been living high & drinking Madeira wine & porter which was my prescription. I have a billet in the most airy part of Lisbon. The Berkeleys have been very attentive to me. You must not be surprised at my drawing

upon you as my living is very expensive but necessary to my health and I have been unfortunate in my horse ... I am not a very good judge. The horse I now have is injured in her shoulder so fear will never recover it.[5]

By 2 September he was back with his regiment. Wellington's troops were then encamped in and around Guarda. His headquarters were again at Celori-

Three small sketches by Francis Simcoe drawn while he was at Leira and the bridge at Murcella, on the Mondego River.

co, and he was preparing to withdraw in good order, hoping to entice a large French force under Marshal Masséna to follow him. Almeida had fallen to the French on 28 August, through treachery, Francis thought. The Portuguese fortress had blown up. The crypt in the cathedral had been used as a powder magazine. Either through carelessness or guile, powder from a keg had left a trail from the square through the building and when ignited had run flame straight to the crypt, with awesome consequences.

Again Francis' division was under orders to move at the shortest notice. As he wrote in many of his letters, he hoped for a packet from home. He was often disappointed because frequently mail had to be forwarded to him and he had missed some letters during his illnesses in Lisbon. When his work was done and the camp quiet, he daydreamed of being near Elizabeth and his sisters, and of telling Henry about his adventures. He had little inclination for some off-duty pleasures of his brother officers. He was at heart the evangelical Anglican his parents had reared. He formed a friendship with the chaplain of the 4th Division, Reverend George Jenkins. However, when the Anglican clergyman talked of being ever in a state of grace, Francis took the council lightly. What officer could lead men effectively if he thought for a moment that he was dashing only to meet his maker?

By 6 September, his division began moving west along the Mondego River towards Coimbra, and Wellington had moved his headquarters closer, to Gouveia again.

Everyone knew that Wellington was retreating to a good purpose, and that he was looking for the perfect spot to challenge Masséna. For Wellington, the time had come to use his secret weapon. The Lines of Torres Vedras were nearly complete, being finished by Portuguese peasant workers now that the soldiers had gone back to war. They were clearing a field of fire before the lines, by removing vegetation that might serve as cover. Wellington wanted two things – a battle he could win, and a retreat during which Masséna's army would be in hostile country, harried by Portuguese *Ordenanza*, partisans, and stripped of food. During the retreat the British and Portuguese troops would be supplied along safe routes from Lisbon or ports north of it.

Wellington stayed at Gouveia until the third week in September while spies informed him of Masséna's advance beyond Almeida, sending his divisions into the hills north of Coimbra and across the Mondego River. He expected Masséna to take the most direct road towards Coimbra and had stationed Rowland Hill's 2nd Division and James Leith's 5th Division on heights above the River Alva that flowed into the Mondego from the south. He expected Masséna to cross the Murcella Bridge. When he found that Masséna had taken the road through Viseu, he decided to meet him around Bussaco, about five miles north of Coimbra. He called back the divisions and chose the great ridge of Bussaco as the perfect place to wait for Masséna. En route Francis'

4th Division had crossed the Murcella Bridge. He enclosed a small sketch of the bridge in a letter home.

The Serra de Bussaco stretched ten miles, aligned north to south, rising from 1,200 to 1,500 feet high. The east-facing slope was very steep and strewn with boulders and clumps of brush. The reverse, or west-facing slope was gentler, but steep enough to conceal his army so that Masséna would not be certain where they were or what their strength. A track ran along the west slope parallel to the crest which Wellington had had improved so that he could move reinforcements quickly if any position was weakened. Two roads extended up the steep eastern slope. The main road to Coimbra ran around the northern end of the ridge and a poorer road went through San Antonio de Cantara and up the centre. The Mondego River wound below cliffs at the southern end of the ridge, overlooked by the hill Nostra Senhora de Monte Alto. South again was the village of Penacova; at the north end where the ridge dipped, was Sula village. The Bussaco Convent, where Wellington would have his headquarters, stood close to the north end of the ridge

Wellington now had 51,000 men, in five numbered Divisions, and the elite Light Division led by the brilliant Robert Crauford, who was Francis' hero. Each division had some Portuguese troops and most brigades had one company of riflemen from the 5th or 6th Battalions 60th, or from the 95th, a rifle regiment. In addition, he had a Portuguese Division, three independent brigades of Portuguese with *Cacadores* (riflemen), two squadons of the 4th Dragoons, and sixty artillery pieces. Half of his army was of Portuguese men.

Francis was bursting with excitement as he marched with the Grenadiers. At last a real fight was imminent. General Cole led the 4th Division to the place Wellington had chosen, at the very north end of the ridge, where it narrowed and the crest overlooked very broken ground. Above Sula was an independent Portuguese brigade, of two regiments of infantry and one of *Cacadores.* Back near the convent were some King's German Legion. In order southwards, stood Robert Crauford's Light Division, then Thomas Picton's 3rd Division, Brent Spencer's 1st Division, James Leith's 5th Division and at the very end Rowland Hill's 2nd Division.

Wellington's command post was just south of the convent where the ground was high. He expected Masséna's approach to be along the Coimbra road, because the road from Viseu led into it. Therefore he put a heavy concentration of troops close together at the north end of the line. By the evening of 25 September his orders had gone out. The officers as well as the men bivouacked near their positions for the night. They ate a cold evening meal on the 26th, without fires although the September night was chilly. In the dark, sleep almost eluded Francis Simcoe.

Masséna's army of 65,000 lit their campfires among the hills to the east. He had three corps – Number II, Marshal Reynier's had two divisions and cavalry.

Marshal Ney commanded Number IV, of three divisions and cavalry. Number VIII, of two divisions and calvalry was under Jean Androche Junot, and would be held back in reserve. The French had 114 guns to Wellington's 60.

The morning of the 27th dawned foggy, but at six o'clock while visibility was still poor, Masséna launched his first attack. Part of Reynier's division marched up the track from San Antonio de Cantaro, between Picton's 3rd Division and Spencer's 1st. Reynier thought that Wellington's entire army would be concentrated more around the road to Coimbra, and from the track he would circle behind the whole army and attack from the rear. Reynier's 14,000 men were repulsed by the divisions, while Leith's and Hill's began to close up to their left. As grape and canister shot poured down from Wellington's four-pounders, Reynier's men broke and ran in disorder. At seven o'clock the second attack, of eleven French battalions against Wellesley's four, was also driven downslope.

Picton's 88th, the Connaught Rangers, had led with a determined volley and charge, followed by the 45th and 74th, also of his 3rd Division. Again zeal sent the French downslope. Wellington's only concern was that his men should not follow too far, where they might not be able to return quickly to the protection of the reverse slope.

With the third assault upslope, the French, weighted down by packs, scrambling through the boulders, nearly got over the crest, but Leith had moved the 5th Division in support of Picton, along the road Wellington had prepared below the crest. Hill, whose instincts told him that Masséna would not come so far south, left his position by Nostra Senora de Monte Alto and moved into the gap. Wellington had won the first phase of the battle. Francis had little idea of what was happening beyond the crash of the guns, staccato of the muskets and rifles, for the dense pall of blue-grey smoke obscured everything.

The fight came closer when Marshal Ney launched IV Corps towards Sula on the main road. He was met by 1,400 British and Portuguese riflemen, and another 1,800 *Cacadores* were standing steady. The Light Division was drawn up out of sight of the French. Robert Crauford set the men in motion with a cry to Sir John Moore's old 52nd to avenge his death. The Light Division swept forward; 1,800 muskets fired at ten paces from the French columns, and 1,800 bayonets charged. Ney sent eleven more battalions to the left but four Battalions of Portuguese who fired steadily forced them to retreat. Masséna had lost 4,600 troops. The British force lost 626, the Portuguese the same number. The 4th Division was entirely unbloodied. Although protected by rough ground of the slope below them, they were strategically placed to tangle with Masséna if he had tried to round the north end along the Coimbra road

The real nightmare for a young subaltern on his first battlefield was the sight and stench of carnage, the cries of the wounded, the bandsmen who acted as stretcher bearers carrying their bloody loads off to the temporary hospital, assisted by men from the ranks. Soldiers and regimental women flowed over the ground, looting anything of value off the dead of both armies, and the wounded too weak to protest. The amount of red blood was incredible

The battle had gone as Wellington had expected, except for a near-mishap His left flank might have been turned in ravines north of Bussaco ridge because the Portuguese had been slow to move into them, an error more embarrassing than serious in an otherwise flawless performance. On the whole the Portuguese had fought as well as the British and other allied troops.

During the night the first of Wellington's men started slipping away, going south to Penacova, at the end of the ridge, then turning west to make their way to the Coimbra road. They wanted to avoid tangling with the French, who would not have expected them to depart by such a roundabout route.[6]

Chapter 16
The Lines of Torres Vedras, Olivenza, Badajoz

R iding south on his not too sound horse, Francis pondered the importance of cavalry. He had just been on the scene of a great battle in
which cavalry hardly was involved. Cavalry could do the devil's work
on a plain, where infantry had to form squares to combat the charges. On Bussaco ridge, with few places where a horse could climb, horses were almost
useless. A four-pounder gun on a hill, firing grape or canister shot, could also
destroy mounted troops more effectively than Wellington's nine pounders
armed with cannon balls. He recalled his father saying that infantry won wars.
He was glad he had chosen a line regiment, even though cavalrymen were
more colourful and they were better at patrolling than foot soldiers.

They marched to Coimbra, one of the few towns from which the inhabitants had not fled taking what possessions they could carry. With the arrival of
the British and Portuguese troops, the people of Coimbra joined the exodus,
clogging the bridge over the Mondego River in their terror of the trailing
French. They left a chaos of burning buildings, an empty prison and a vacant
lunatic hospital, so that the populace fleeing for Lisbon embraced the good,
bad and unfortunate. At Coimbra occurred the famous incident when Wellington ordered his rules against looting enforced. While hanging a soldier caught
with a huge mirror, Wellington ordered the Provost Marshal to hang the mirror
beside the culprit, as a warning to the rest of the army.

Men in England who were critical of Wellington were quick to say that he
had retreated in defeat, but Francis knew that his chief was leading his army to
safety, to be ready to fight when he could win. Masséna's army was following
them, and the Portuguese militia and *Ordenanza* were making their way north
to harass him. Word arrived that Masséna's troops had looted Coimbra thoroughly, and that the Marshal had left 5,000 sick and wounded men who lay on
straw sacks around a hospital that could not accommodate even a fraction of
them. Francis wondered at Masséna's motives. He must have been thinking
that he would chase Wellington into the streets of Lisbon, and force another
British evacuation as at Corunna. He would be in for a surprise when the
British and Portuguese marched between the many forts and around obstacles

and earthworks. Once they passed through the Lines of Torres, Masséna would never be allowed to follow.

While Wellington led his army south, Colonel Nicholas Trant, an Irishman who led Portuguese light troops, moved on Coimbra, where his vengeful followers wrought havoc on the 5,000 helpless Frenchmen Masséna had deserted. Added to Trant's men and the Portuguese soldiers, *Ordenanza*

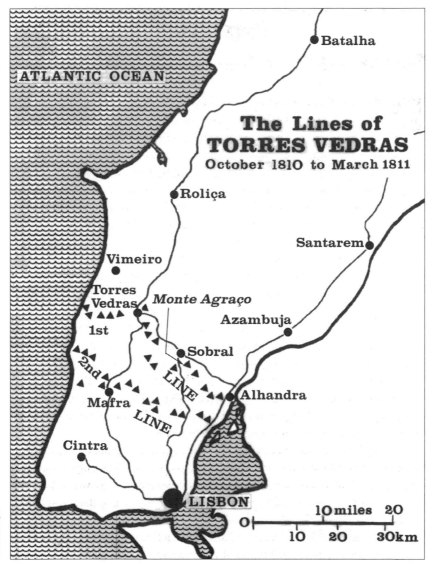

flowed in behind Masséna and his army, cutting off all communication with France. Masséna, Francis knew, in going forward, was walking into Wellington's trap, but he was perhaps not aware that Masséna could not retreat either. To the north the Portuguese blocked him. Masséna was thinking, if he could take Lisbon he would be able to provision his army. No food could reach him from France, and he had taken all the bread to be found at Almeida. His army was already starving in the empty scorched countryside.

Francis had not yet seen the Lines of Torres Vedras, but there was no end of gossip among the officers. He had heard more than most of them because of being ill in Lisbon, where everyone knew that Wellington was building something extraordinary just up the road. He had caught glimpses of some of the workings as he rode back to Guarda in late August. The 4th Division was marching a day behind Wellington. On 8 October Wellington entered the Lines of Torres Vedras, and directed the troops to enter in two file lines. He had designated which divisions, brigades or battalions would go to each of some 152 forts, and long lines of men moved slowly towards them. Lowry Cole was to take his 4th Division as far as Sobral, in the first line. They were in place on 9 October, and the entire operation of feeding the troops into their designated places had gone smoothly. By 10 October, the entire army was within the Lines, except for cavalry patrols out keeping track of Masséna.[1]

The next day Francis saw some action. Masséna's vanguard attacked in force the pickets of the 4th Division around the Sobral position. Before they had suffered much damage the 4th Division withdrew in good order three miles to a fortified camp on the heights of Monte Agraco. The mountain towered high above all the others in the area. The men of the 4th Division, and others stationed at Agraco, would have had a clear view of Sobral, once the skies cleared. Rain had been falling constantly since Wellington had arrived on the 8th, but it had worked in their favour. Streams were overflowing their banks, impeding Masséna's progress.

On the 14th Masséna reached Sobral. Marshal Junot went forth and occupied some of the outer defences, where he saw enough to recognize just how impregnable Wellington's position was. Masséna rode to look for himself, as far as Fort 120 at the eastern end of the Lines. A soldier fired a warning shot, and Masséna galloped away. He would remain at Sobral for a month. He dared not risk repeating the fiasco at Bussaco.

On 19 October, Francis wrote a description of the position to Elizabeth:

> You must by this time have received my letter with the account of the battle of Busaco … and the lengthy account of our retreat must be given when I have a little more news. I know a lot of it sufficed to say though how we have arrived at our fatal position which is to guide this country at least for the present … we have retreated to about 5 or 6 leagues from Lisbon on a range of hills that extend from Bella Franca to Agraco and in

a post which is thought to be stronger than any other part of the position. We have 24 pieces of cannon on the heights

He hoped that the French would approach them, but they were not showing their force as a whole as they had at Bussaco. Thus far the French were staying put at Sobral:

> There was a smart skirmish the day before yesterday [17 October] which ended greatly in our favour – as usual we have an immense force here all supplied and provisioned and are never in the rear of our position & the enemy can have none but which they brought with them. Their wounded, sick & prisoners have all been sent to Coimbra so that their supplies are entirely cut off and I think myself they must be in a very bad way for we are much astonished at their waiting so long without attacking us at the first opportunity.

He supposed they were waiting for reinforcements. He had heard that Admiral Berkeley had been made Lord High Admiral of Portugal, news that was certain to please his mother.

Writing on 26 November, he reminded Elizabeth that he had not heard from her for a long time. He was now at Azambuja, close to the first line, and twenty miles down the road from Santarem:

> The French troops are cantonned at Santarem. We hope for constant skirmishes with the enemy & prisoners and deserters pass through [on their way to Lisbon]. What surprises us most is from whence they draw provisions as we know the commissaries are cut off on all quarters, nor have they as yet attempted to open them. We are well provisioned with the exception that the beef is intolerably bad from want of forage for the bullocks & for my own part I do not know where or when the campaign will end. The French left their position near Sobral in a great hurry as we judge from their huts. I went to see many of them, they are better suited [than ours] to the inclemency of the weather. We found meat and tender corn & found the French books which they were unable to take away in their hurry & bustle of a sudden movement. I found in the hut of an officer of rank what seemed to be from its appearance a letter from Masséna's Adjut. Genl ... dated Nov. 11th not to permit any of the troops to leave their cantonments on any account under pain of severe punishiment as the Prince of Essling, Commander in Chief intended to review the Army on Nov. 12th. It is rather extraordinary that the Prince [would not know the situation]. The Prince instead on the 12th of reviewing them moved off as fast as he possibly could march and entrenched,

having left the heights, at Santarem. We found on the road numbers
of dead Frenchmen, mules, horses broken down.[2]

Francis referred to Masséna by the title, Prince of Essling, awarded to him
by Napoleon. The emperor was creating a new aristocracy, as a final blow to
the aspirations of the French Revolution.

The once beautiful town of Azambuja, Francis was sorry to write, was a
mess. Upon arrival they took charge of the sick and the very numerous prisoners. Francis found, in one of the regimental records dated there, that 662 were
in hospital out of a regiment of 1,900. He knew that a box had arrived for him
in Lisbon, but he had only six or eight dollars, not enough to have it sent. He
just hoped it was not something from somebody "valuable." At that time the
recipient of a letter or parcel paid the postage. In closing he reported that there
had been a change in the 4th Division recently. Colonel John Harvey's two
battalions of Portuguese troops had been added.[3]

He wrote again, on 22 December, very happy that he had received one from
Elizabeth, but disappointed that an important letter he had sent had been lost:

> I was much dispirited at your not receiving mine about Busaco, as it gave
> you a lot of information respecting that, but however I am saving an
> account of the detail for Eliza but will not delay sending this letter as you
> may be anxious to hear from me.

He was sorry to hear such a bad account of the Old King, and hoped the
country would not lose him at such a time as the present. The armies were in
the same position as they had been for some time, but he thought the campaign
would soon end. He did not say why, but he was certain the French had no
choice and would have to withdraw into Spain or starve to death. In fact,
Masséna had already lost hundreds to malnutrition and related diseases. The
27th Regiment, with some others, had moved from Azambuja to a filthy village on the north bank of the Tagus. The woods had plenty of game to shoot,
but there were no dogs to act as retrievers.

That they were finding any game at all was odd. The French had been
scouring that very area not too long before and they must have taken anything
that moved. He was finding the weather remarkably fine, and provisions plentiful and not too expensive considering the "times & circumstances. I am
obliged to scribble in a great hurry to be in time for this post. N.B. I received
the box, from Hackets Whitehall, for which I paid 7 dollars."[4]

He did not say what it contained, but Elizabeth had arranged to send several things he asked for. Besides a chess set she had sent to Lisbon, he had a
Portuguese grammar, and a dictionary which he used frequently. He had not
had the opportunity to learn enough Spanish to write to Miss Burges, but he
could make himself understood at Torres Vedras. Some of his letters continued

to be almost too faint to decipher because the quality of most of the paper available in a war-torn country was so poor.

The bulk of the British army remained within the lines of Torres Vedras until March, but Wellington ordered the regiments, brigades and divisions to be constantly on the move. Francis named many places where he had stopped only briefly. The Lines of Torres Vedras were not continuous; the individual fortresses, gun emplacments and redoubts were not joined together by linking walls. Thus two files of soldiers could march everywhere unobstructed. The Lines were also manned by Portuguese militia. These remained in set positions, but Wellington wanted his better trained regular units to be able to reinforce any spot that might be threatened by Masséna.

In order for them to do so, Wellington had them constantly moving from one position to a new one. He wanted all his officers to memorize the whole fortified structure so that if they were called upon to move anywhere, they would be able to obey instantly without misleading their men or getting lost themselves. The 27th Regiment was at a different location almost every night, sometimes on its own, with the brigade, or marching with the entire 4th Division. For a time the division was above Ajambuja, so close to the French pickets that when on patrol, men from both sides called out greetings to each other.[5]

On 5 March Masséna began to withdraw his starving army from Santarem, which took him until 8 April. In the meantime Wellington had moved some of his battalions out of the Lines of Torres Vedras. On 4 March Francis wrote Elizabeth from Castello Branco, which was nearly 200 miles outside the outermost Line. The 4th Division was marching south towards the Tagus. A report circulated that Marshal Auguste Marmont was marching parallel to them on the south side of the river with seven divisions. "I rather think we shall have some hot work this summer."[6] Thus far, the 4th Division was part of a force with orders to prevent a junction between Marmont and Masséna.

By that time Wellington had divided his army into two parts. He was leading the northern part, following Masséna, who was moving towards Almeida and Ciudad Rodrigo. The 4th Division had been with the northern part, but was soon to move southwards towards the Alentejo (a province in south central Portugal).[7]

The second part, Wellington had placed under the command of General William Beresford, who was marching towards Badajoz. Marshal Soult was laying siege to the fortress. The Marquess de la Romano, the only Spanish general Wellington trusted, had died in January, and he feared the worst. He dispatched the 2nd and 4th Divisions to reinforce Beresford. In addition to the two British Divisions, Beresford's army included a Portuguese Division, two independent brigades, one German and one Portuguese, and more than 2,000 British and Portuguese cavalry. Once the various divisions had assembled, Beresford would be in command of more than 20,000 men. Wellington knew he could not take the offensive into Spain until he controlled both Badajoz and

Almeida. He had to protect the first and capture the second. On 11 March the Spanish surrendered at Badajoz, and the French marched into the walled town and the most impregnable of the border defences.

Now Wellington instructed Beresford to lay siege to Badajoz, to dislodge the French from the other fortress necessary to a British advance. By 20 March, Francis was in the Alentejo. On the 25th the Divisions joined Beresford at Campo Maior, where he drew out some of the allowance Elizabeth allowed him. They marched to Olivenza, an outpost of Badajoz some thirty miles to the southeast where, on 9 April, the governor of the fort refused to surrender. Beresford marched on towards Albuera, leaving General Cole and the 4th Division and a regiment of Portuguese cavalry to reduce Olivenza. The Division quickly invested the little fortress. A detachment of Royal Artillery arrived, after hauling some siege guns from Elvas. On 11 April Cole's men seized a detached lunette the French had evacuated, and strengthened it so that it could be used as a springboard for an assault. A lunette consisted of two faces forming a salient angle (a bulge arranged so that soldiers inside could provide crossfire) and two parallel flank walls. Under weak fire from the fort, a party set about cutting a passage into the lunette through the salient angle, which faced the Division. The men had some protection from French fire by the flank walls and by earthwork behind the lunette. The working party completed the works by the 14th. On the 15th Cole called upon the fort to surrender.[8]

When the French did not deign to reply, the guns opened up with round shot to breach the curtain wall of their fort. Meanwhile, at a safe distance back, the troops were perfecting their musket drill and the officers were making tentative plans to storm the breach if the French were stubborn. Volunteers were asking to join the forlorn hope, the first who would enter the breach. Francis was tempted to ask to lead it, but he knew he would not receive permission. He would not be twenty for another three months, and he had only been a subaltern for three years. He had to have served four years before he could be considered for a captaincy. Leading a forlorn hope and surviving meant certain promotion, without purchase. If he could spare his mother the price of a captaincy he would be very proud of himself. Cole tentatively chose a lieutenant who had served the four years. Francis would have to wait until he had put in the time. Then, even if he did not have the seniority, as the hero of a forlorn hope he might jump the queue.

The firing from the Royal Artillery ceased when the governor of the fort asked for a meeting under a flag of truce. Cole rejected his terms and demanded unconditional surrender. The firing resumed, threatening to enlarge the breach, until the governor agreed to Cole's terms. The breach would not be stormed after all. Inside were 480 men and 12 pieces of artillery. A detachment of Portuguese and the Royal Artillerymen was detailed to haul the captured guns towards Badajoz, where they could be turned on the enemy. On the 16th the 4th Division marched from its bivouac near Olivenza through the Alentejo and the whole force was soon gathered at Zafre. During the siege Francis had had no time to write. If he wrote an account later it was lost, but this had been his first opportunity to take part in a siege.

On 30 April he wrote from a place he called Montijo, where some of the troops gathered around Campo Maior were staying. At a river Kemmis' Brigade had been stopped by rising water that had washed away a bridge. The 27th and 97th Regiments had already crossed over it, but the 40th Regiment and the baggage brigade were marooned on the opposite bank. Those who had crossed had now been eight days without any baggage, which was being sent round to another bridge. They were desperate for their belongings:

> I went with another officer & across the river in a sort of boat ... After some distance of a bright moon [we] got our baggage on four horses ... and swam our animals & was very happy to get it ... Obliged to lay in bed to get our linen washed. ... There is an amphitheatre well worth seeing, it is six leagues distant. From Campo Maior to this place is a beautiful plain covered with corn & the ground so very rich... We lay 1 or 2 nights in a wood at Albuera of immense extent. After fording two rivers up to our [knees] everything is progressing as quick as possible for besieging Badajoz. There are about 2000 men in it. Ld Wellington was here a few days since looking extremely well.[9]

He closed his letter with, "I am on guard and must be off."

Wellington could not afford to remain long advising Beresford. He had left the northern army in the hands of General Sir Brent Spencer and he was anxious to resume personally the command of the force following Masséna. Marshal Soult was somewhere to the south. After Badajoz fell he had departed leaving what he assumed to be a garrison large enough to repel attackers. Apparently he had no intention of reinforcing Masséna. No love was lost between these two Marshals of Napoleon's, a fact of which Wellington was apprised. As he left, Wellington hoped that Beresford had the capacity to take Badajoz before a warning could be relayed to Soult.

By eight o'clock on the morning of 8 May, the 4th Division reached Badajoz and took up a position on the opposite bank of the Guardiana River. The honeysuckers were back.

Three days before, Wellington had inflicted a defeat on Masséna at a village called Fuentes de Onoro. From secure Ciudad Rodrigo, the French Marshal had met Wellington on one of His Lordship's favourite sites – a ridge, steep slope facing the enemy, a more gentle reverse slope where he could keep his strength concealed. A new, inexperienced 7th Division, fresh out from Britain, had almost met disaster, but Robert Crauford skillfully led his Light Division. By an intricate pattern of form square to force the enemy back, and quick march by column, then another square when Masséna's men again drew near, and another march by column, rescued the 7th. At Fuentes de Onoro, Wellington had 38,000 men and 40 guns to Masséna's 48,000 men and 48 guns. He lost 1,400 to Masséna's 2,250.

Chapter 17
Acting Captain Francis Simcoe

The town of Badajoz was surrounded by a thick masonry wall thirty feet high or better, crowned on the landward sides by eight bastions (all with saints' names except the Trinidad, equally appropriate for Catholic Spain). The castle stood on a cliff 100 feet high at the northeast corner, overlooking the Guardiana River. A stone bridge linked the north and south banks of the Guardiana. A tributary, the Rivillas River, flowed into the Guardiana along the east wall. Looking across the wide Guardiana, Francis Simcoe surveyed the scene with fresh eyes. The last time he had been here, the garrison was of Spanish allies, hostile ones, but less deadly than the present inmates. He studied a map Colonel Maclean had loaned to the junior officers.

As well as the heavily armed walled town, he noted the Tête de Pont Fort, at the exit to the bridge where the road from Elvas crossed it. To the south was the Pardaleras Fort, guarding the approach from Albuera. Across the Rivillas River lay the small St. Roque Lunette and the much more formidable Picurina Fort. Closest to the Division's encampment was the San Cristobal Fort. It would have to be taken before any action could proceed against the town. The 4th Division was sent to join the troops on the north side of the Guardiana, where Major General William Lumley was the commanding officer. Francis described an action the day after they arrived:

> Our [Kemmis'] brigade was joined by the 17th Portuguese of the line which with a few militia & Artillery composed the whole of our force on this side of the Guardiana. On the 9th we dislodged the Enemy's picquets & drove them within their post, sustaining but a small loss. I was sent out on picquet duty with [another officer] who commanded. Genl Lumley who commands on this side ... was much pleased with the style in which we drove them, in tho exposed to a severe fire from the batteries, but fortunately had only ten of our picket wounded.

> In case you should not be aware of the situation at Badajoz I shall describe it to you as concisely as possible. On this side is St. Christoval;

it is on a height about 400 yds from the bridge. At this end of the bridge there is the Tete de Pont Fort.[1]

They had been on working parties, preliminary to laying siege to San Cristobal. Because Captain John Pring was off with one working party, Lieutenant Charles Levinge had charge of the company, then 49 strong because so many were away on duty. They were part of a force of 500 men, probably the wing of the 27th that Major John Birmingham had been leading, that went into action with detachments of other regiments of Kemmis' Brigade. Some of the troops succeeded in driving the French out of a battery, but with considerable loss. At some point John Pring returned, and took over. When they advanced they were opposed in the first instance by a squadron of cavalry and 600 infantrymen "whom we drove before us in great style pushing the men and horses although under the fire ... from the guns of San Chrisvobal, Tete de Pont and the Town."

Major Birmingham was severely wounded in the beginning of the action, of which he died yesterday, as was also Captain Pring & Lt. Levinge so that the command of the Company devolved on me. Very early in the action after the fall of Major Birmingham, who just before said he would enter Badajoz with the French troops, I was sent to drive out some French who were pressing us, which place I soon drove them off ... The Brigade lost some 600 between killed and wounded.

He recalled Major Birmingham as a most gallant officer. "I am happy to tell you though Capt. Pring is severely wounded that I am in great hopes he will recover, he is in good spirits & bears it with a manly fortitude."

He asked me to mention that he was wounded but not dangerously which you have the goodness to communicate, assuring them from me that I will let them know constantly how he is going on & that I shall give him every assistance that is in my power. He is a man for whom I have a great esteem on his own, as well as other considerations, he is generally loved by everybody that knows him. Poor Maj. Birmingham was a particular friend. I believe Col. Mclean was wounded yesterday .... At present may the almighty God who protected me through so many dangers protect my dear Mother and family.[2]

P.S. Genl Lumley has spoken of us in the highest terms in general & has promised to report it in the strongest manner to Marshall Beresford. I am sure the Brigade deserves it, for great gallentry, hardiness & intrepidity never was witnessed.

The attempt to storm San Cristobal was a major event at the first siege of Badajoz. The losses were heavy. While Francis' account is not that clear, it is not only an eye-witness one, but that of a very involved participant. From the moment the command of the Grenadier Company fell to him, he was bound and determined to find a way to keep it. He knew that John Pring would require a very long time to recover from his wounds, and would be going

The Royal Inniskilling Fusiliers Regimental Museum, Enniskillen, Northern Ireland.

The Second Siege of Badajoz, June 1811.

home soon. Charles Levinge, too, would not mend quickly. Francis remembered his mother telling him how long it had taken his father to recover from the wounds he suffered in the Revolutionary War, especially those he sustained at the Battle of Brandywine. He would be commanding the company indefinitely, as long as the army did not have a spare captain to send to the Grenadiers.

In his version, General Lowry Cole viewed events from a wider perspective. General Beresford had invested Badajoz on 5 May, and commenced the first serious siege undertaken by the British army in the Peninsula. The Right Brigade of the 4th Division was detached with troops of the 2nd Division to act against San Cristobal. "Ground was broke on the 8th of May, before the fort of St. Christoval, on the right of the Guardiana, and on the day following before [in front of] the body of the place, on the left bank of the river."[3]

The army was ill prepared to conduct a siege. The tools were in short supply and of poor quality. The men did not know how to make approaches by trenching, and the army still had no sappers and miners to perform part of the work and give direction to the soldiers. The guns were antiques brought from the walls of Elvas, which hardly damaged the wall of San Cristobal. Before the walls could be breached, Beresford received word, on 13 May, that Marshal Soult was marching in force to relieve Badajoz. Beresford departed with most of his army towards Albuera. He left General Cole and his 4th Division, and General Harvey's Portuguese brigade, behind to cover the removal of guns and stores. The French made a sortie on the afternoon of the 14th, to establish how many troops Beresford had left behind. The 4th Division, which Cole had moved across the Guardiana, nearer the town, lined up behind the wretched artillery pieces, and the French immediately sought the shelter of the walls.

Beresford resolved to wait for Soult at Albuera. There, on the night of the 15th, he was joined by 14,000 men in two Spanish corps under the command of Generals Blake and Castanos. Blake was Spanish, of Irish descent, a reminder that some fugitives had fled to Spain as a result of the Rebellion of 1798. With the arrival of the Spanish, Beresford's force numbered 38,000 men. Soult was coming with 25,000. If Wellington had been there, the odds would have been in Britain's favour, even though nearly a third of the force was Spanish, whose officers and men had consistently let their allies down. In the field Beresford was no Wellington.

Beresford was soon in trouble. The 2nd Division, serving with General William Stewart because General Rowland Hill was ill, had been badly mauled. Colonel John Colborne's brigade of light troops had almost been wiped out. Beresford sent a message to General Cole to bring part of his division to Albuera as quickly as possible. Cole chose his brigade of Fusiliers, one company of the 1st Battalion 23rd Regiment and 1st and 2nd Battalions of the 7th (Francis' grandfather Gwillim's onetime corps). Cole took only three companies from Kemmis' Brigade – the Light Companies of the 27th, 40th and 97th. The rest were two regiments of Harvey's Portuguese Brigade, and the 1st Battalion, Loyal Lusitanian Legion. Francis was crushed. Here might have been the chance to prove that he was as good as any captain at ordering the volleys, drawing his sabre and leading a bayonet charge once the enemy had been softened up by musket fire. He turned to the more mundane task of directing the men at moving the guns and supplies. He felt even worse when he learned that Lowry Cole had won the Battle of Albuera for William Beresford.

The tale of how Cole succeeded varied with the narrator. Henry Hardinge, a future governor general of India, was deputy quartermaster general at Albuera. Hardinge suggested that Cole, waiting with the reserves, take his men to the right of the Portuguese to protect the flank from that direction. Others maintained that the idea of joining the fray was Cole's own. Whatever the truth, Cole acted without orders. He set off with only his Brigade of Fusiliers. His Fusiliers provided the dash required to chase Soult from the field. Soult numbered his losses at 8,000, among them five generals. Of 7,640 British who were engaged, 3,930 were casualties. Cole himself had been wounded, but not seriously.[4] The only comfort to Francis was the return of the Light Company of the 27th, who never left the reserves. If he had been there with his Grenadiers, he, too, would have had to stand and watch. At least he had been useful to Colonel Maclean, whose wound was healing nicely and he was back on duty.

On 19 May, Lord Wellington arrived at Badajoz to resume the siege. On the 11th, Almeida had fallen to his northern army, although to his fury, the French garrison had escaped. The Portuguese fortress, in poor shape after the explosion before the French took it, now had a garrison of allied troops who had started rebuilding it. Marshal Masséna had been recalled, and Marshal Marmont was in command of Ciudad Rodrigo. Wellington intended taking Badajoz, then turning on Marmont. With him came General Rowland Hill, now recovered. Wellington gave Hill, who had many times proved his worth, the command of the southern army. Beresford returned to training the Portuguese, for which he was better suited.

The same day, 19 May, the army began attempting to force a breach through the main wall of Badajoz. Francis celebrated his twentieth birthday on 6 June. He was contented that his Grenadiers were becoming skilled at skirmishing with French parties that came out of the fortress. When they were allotted tools, they joined working parties attempting to build trenches about the walls. They had to take turns because there were not nearly enough spades to go round. Tools captured from the French were vastly superior and much coveted. Again Wellington was lamenting the dearth of sappers and miners to inspire the soldiers.

By 10 June, Wellington had decided the task was hopeless, and he ordered a withdrawal to Elvas. Without guns powerful enough to break the walls, his troops could not attack the garrison. He would have to postpone the taking of Badajoz until he could bring up a proper siege train from the coast. Siege guns, 18 and 24-pounders, alone could admit him into the town. Even then he would need a very much larger army which, he knew, would suffer horrendous casualties.

On 21 June 1811, Francis wrote from camp at Toro de Moro that he was waiting anxiously for a letter from home before writing, but though a packet had arrived the day before none of the letters were for him:

We are hutted in a small wood about 2 leagues from Elvas, 1 league from Campo Maior, where we have been since the 19th. You will have been disappointed to know that we were obliged a second time to retreat [from] the siege of Badajoz and return across the Guardiana, everybody here was [grim] … saying that we were going to the line but it is now quite changed. We expect every day to move on again. We had a skirmish on the 20th in which we took a number of prisoners but unfortunately lost one Capt., 1 Lieut & 45 of the 11th Lt. Dragoons.[5]

He enquired whether Elizabeth had heard from Lord Moira of late, and whether he had said anything about a captaincy:

I know he told me when I was in London that he was to get it for me as soon as a subaltern that was now expired some time and as I am nearly four years a subaltern as I look upon a Company as the most important step n the army. Until you arrive at that you can very very seldom have an opportunity of gaining any credit. Promotion is now regulated in such a manner that it must take a long time before a man can [have hope] of getting a promotion.[6]

He understood that in the regular course of events in the 27th Regiment, he might have to wait at least twelve years before he was senior enough:

I remember mentioning in a letter to Eliza some time ago that I hoped I should get my Company. She wrote me back that I should not be in a hurry, that I was not aware of the change [in the rules], of that I am perfectly aware.

Eliza had counselled him to write to Lord Moira, as a reminder, but not to make his letter too obvious.

He was in a hurry. By 30 October he would have been four years a subaltern. He believed that there was no time like the present to arouse Lord Moira's awareness that his Ensign's commission had been signed on 30 October 1807. When he went to visit John Pring, who was about to be sent home, he questioned him about the possibility of success. John Graves Simcoe had become a captain after four years from the day he joined the army as an ensign. Pring counted back. True, but the General had been nineteen when he entered the army, not sixteen. He got his captaincy at age twenty-three. He felt that Francis would not have to wait twelve years, not with a war on that was murdering or disabling captains rapidly. Pring was reassuring. Surely, by the time Francis reached twenty-three he would qualify in every respect. Pring was looking forward to going home, and he promised to have his family invite Mrs. Simcoe to visit without delay, so that he could give her a full account of him. Francis pretended to be comforted, but even four years was farther into the future than he could accept.

By the end of June Wellington had resolved on his next move. He would bottle up Marmont in Ciudad Rodrigo and fight him until he had forced the French Marshal to surrender the fortress. Wellington left a garrison at Elvas, sufficient, he trusted, to keep Soult from attacking it, and moved his headquarters north, close to Almeida. At Elvas Francis began putting together more of his journal for Eliza. The Division had marched west to Estremoz, then north to Portalagre and on towards Castello Branco. At times the summer heat was almost beyond endurance. Summer was the season of drought when rain almost never fell. "I remember an unfortunate Portuguese soldier of the 11th who was exceptionally fatigued from the heat. He lay himself down in the road as he was so ill from the heat." They reached Vila Velha de Rodao on 5 August. By the 6th they were at Castello Branco. They went into encampment at the tiny village of Aldea do Obispo, almost on the Spanish border a short distance north of Fuentes de Onoro, reputed to be the site of one of Wellington's bloodier triumphs.

On 12 August he wrote to Elizabeth, thanking her for letters she had sent from Seaton and Ashfield (the home of Mary Anne Burges). The regiments were cantonned in several small villages in the vicinity. The reason why the army was now so scattered was for secrecy. Wellington did not want Marmont to obtain a full picture of who was where:

I am happy to hear so good an account of Capt. Pring. I will have you send the enclosed to him. I am glad to hear a better account of Miss Burges, such an affliction to have... the King's recovery is at an end.[7]

He had written Lord Moira, as Eliza had suggested:

I should be very happy to get my Co. in any regiment although it would be satisfactory for me to get it in the 27th as I know could if it had been possible I should get the Grenadier Co. which is vacant & likely to be so for some time. I see R. England has got his Co. He is certainly a fortunate young man.

He referred to Richard England Jr., whose father, Richard England Sr., had been the Lieutenant Colonel Commandant of the 24th Foot when it had been stationed at Detroit back in 1793. Francis had met Richard Jr. while they were small boys in Upper Canada. When they met in Portugal they exchanged greetings although they did not know each other well.

On 18 August, Francis had stopped the journal to Eliza and had written again to Elizabeth. He had written so often of late that he had little news:

It is now reported that Ciudad Rodrigo is certainly to be invested, and we are to take up a position between that place and Salamanca. There was a small detachment of the 12th Dragoons taken the other day. Our cavalry are not up to the [mark] in outpost duty. The report is that we move at the beginning of the month or latter end of this. I have just received a letter from Captn Pring as I wrote to him a few days ago. I shall not answer it now. Remember me to Harriett for her July 20th letter.[8]

By 3 September he was at Castillejo de Martin Viejo, Spain, twenty miles northwest of Ciudad Rodrigo. He was in a very small village, one league inside Spain, not far from Fort Conception, and close to the left of Lord Wellington's position at the battle of 5 May at Fuentes de Onoro. They had marched close by the fort, which they found almost blown out of the earth:

> Several of the frontier towns and other villages through which they had marched were entirely destroyed, houses unroofed and churches destroyed. We arrived here yesterday and from the [state] of the village we are so crowded that I have been obliged to make myself a shade with a blanket, there being no trees near the village. I wish to give you an account of our route.[9]

He proceeded to give distances in leagues, to villages that were very small or no longer exist. They passed through some country so barren that "you could not suppose yourself in a civilized country." At one point, when they were close to Fuentes de Onoro, he made a detour by himself to study the battle ground. When he came to the Coa River, which flowed north past Almeida to empty into the Mondego, he stopped for a swim. As he half expected the site of the battle was a ridge behind which Wellington had concealed his army while the French faced the steep slope from the the plain below and had to wade across the shallow Dos Casas stream. Fuentes de Onoro lay sprawled across the only accessible part of the steep slope. Viewing it Francis understood why the battle had been such a bloody one. The walls of the many stone cottages, now in ruins, had provided cover for both sides. Fuentes de Onoro had been a nasty street fight.

By 3 September they had reached Villa Toro, where they lay in bivouac. They had been sleeping in the open for some time as not much accommodation was to be found in the rugged near no-man's-land in border country. They expected to stay some time, but at three o'clock in the morning they received the order to march and at four the next afternoon they stopped at another poor village:

> I am in hopes we shall leave this place to get more room as we have two Regiments in about 30 hovels. There is a pretty high wind and no convenience but my knee which must plead for all inaccuracies but there is a mail going for England immediately and I do not like to lose the opportunity … I was much disappointed the day before we left Aldea del Obsipo by an officer telling me I was promoted to a Co. in Ireland positively. He saw my name in the gazette which afterwards turned out to be a mistake what made me think it more likely not expect it so soon yet his positive assertion on my thinking it not improbable raised my expectations to a very big pitch.

The captaincy dominated his thoughts as Wellington was concentrating his army ever closer to Ciudad Rodrigo. Elizabeth had enclosed a letter Lord Moira had sent her. Francis was grateful but, he had heard, the only chance he knew of attaining a captaincy would be when he was the senior lieutenant in the army for purchase. That would likely take some years. He may have been toying with the idea of applying to lead a forlorn hope, but he would never have put such a thought into his mother's head. "We shall have an immense force of cavalry here in a short time which will greatly facilitate our movements."[10]

On 19 September he wrote to Charlotte:

I have just received your long & affectionate letter of Aug. 29th ... your letters are always so long & affectionate and afford me so much amusement that I should be very much to blame if I did not take the earliest opportunity of answering it. We are in the same situation for a long time ... The report is that the French are advancing to relieve Ciudad Rodrigo but it is much doubted whether they have a force at all adequate to the effort, and they have not a force equal to our own there is no doubt.

He reiterated what he had written their mother, that with Lord Moira's help he might not have to wait too long for a company. Richard England had been farther down the list than he, which was proof that he might not be surprised "to see within a course of a few gazettes, anything the contrary would be a disappointment." He almost knew his time was to be short:

I fear I should be an old man grey headed and unfit for service if I lived so long, that is, I mean by regular [steps] of promotion was it quicker than it has been the last few years in this Reg't.

Coll Maclean joined us in the last town. We are settled in near Fort Conception. He paid me a very flattering compliment. He said that having heard I was likely to get a Co. and that I chose remaining in this Regt under which circumstances if I had the least idea of joining he would keep the Grenadier Co. open for me.

I could not but be highly sensitive of the compliments & when I have a chance of the command of any Co. in the army I believe it would be it as I so thoroughly know it & the men are much attached to me.[11]

By 3 October he was at Nave de Haver, just inside the border of Portugal. Again he reported the houses in the villages were destroyed. Rain was pouring down in torrents, the wind was very high and the atmosphere dark. The village stood on a bleak plain. The 97th Regiment was leaving shortly for England, but as he did not know that any of them were from Devonshire he would not send letters with them.

From Nave de Haver he wrote to Harriet. Their mother had reported Harriet in poor health, and he hoped soon for a better account. He could not remember whether he owed the letter to Sophia or Harriet, but as he was worried about her he decided that Sophia could wait:

> I have written to Caroline an account of our late movements and I have since written to my Mother whereof. I am afraid I shall not be able to make it so entertaining a letter as I could wish, however you must take the will for the deed and that it is more the idea of writing to please you plus any real pleasure I can give you by my writing.

He had forgotten to mention in his last letter home "of a narrow escape that happened to our noble Commander in Chief." His regiment was in close column at the time and "under severe cannonade with nothing but a few trees and some broken rocks could have hindered us suffering very materially" when he spotted two heroic commanders:

> Ld Wellington and Genl Cole were a short distance to our left on a small height and as is often the case with the former was too exposed when a shell burst between the two Generals. How they could have both escaped affected us, the circumstances were extraordinary as fortunate that he always escapes considering he exposes himself to so much.... He would be a severe loss to this country.[12]

He had a very handsome cartouche (cartridge) box that he assumed had belonged to some French officer of rank. The lid was embroidered in gold with a handsome eagle and an Imperial worked on the cover. He would send it home when he had the opportunity. It had been brought to him by one of his Grenadiers, who was on picket duty when he noticed a corpse in a French uniform and went looking for something of value. The body had been plundered of everything except the handsome box which lay underneath it. Francis did not disapprove. The men were paid little enough, and plundering corpses was part of army life. In fact, he was touched that his man had made him a present of the box instead of selling it or keeping it for himself.

Chapter 18
Coimbra 1811 and Ciudad Rodrigo 1812

In his journal, Francis warned his family not to be taken in by rumours of French successes in the skirmishing with Wellington.

Reports that Wellington had been defeated, either by Masséna, who as far as was known was back in France, or the "General Marshall of Rayusa" who in French reports had driven the allied armies from their positions. In fact Marshal Auguste Marmont, dubbed Duke of Rayusa by Napoleon, had been driven from some of his own heights and Wellington was safe at his latest headquarters, at Freneda, close to Fuendes de Onoro and convenient to Almeida He was firmly entrenched, surrounded by a growing army. Marmont, not His Lordship, had been obliged to evacuate his position:

> but as usual in the French bombastic style, you will hear that the English were defeated & driven across [the Coa], serves as contradictory as may appear to find us advancing to within a few miles of the fortress of Ciudad Rodrigo ...

The sun was shining, it was so beautiful that he was in a romantic mood. On a whim, he wondered whether he should switch from writing a journal to a romance, a novel. "I must now end this letter with praying that the Almighty may grant of his infinite goodness better health & happiness to my own Dear & affectionate Sister Harriet." He asked to be remembered to Henry, Mother and Sisters.[1]

By 6 November Francis was in Celorico, one of Wellington's former headquarters. "I am relieved from my Detachment at Almeida and am now on my way to Coimbra with the Regt for our clothing." He spoke volumes. Apparently this was the first time the 27th Regiment would be refitted, after two years in the field. The men would have been appallingly tattered and threadbare and seriously in want of footwear. The camp women resorted to mending with coarse brown cloth woven by Portuguese peasants, to keep the uniforms at least free of holes in embarrassing places. Some commanders were fussy about the

appearance of their troops, but performance, not appearance, was all that counted with Wellington. (In the Canadas after 1812, the year the United States
declared war on Britain, Commander in Chief Sir George Prevost proved that
he was no Wellington. Through conservative defensive policies he saved the
Canadas, but he demanded spit and polish of his soldiers.)

Carriages were not available, but Francis did not say how they were travelling. Most likely they were on foot, with whatever baggage they were bringing going on boats down the Mondego River. The men rebuilding the fortifications at Almeida were getting on well, important because of the threat by Marmont's troops in Ciudad Rodrigo. "We are only waiting now for provisions so
I have not time for a long letter, you shall hear more from Coimbra."[2]

He was destined to have an extended stay at Coimbra "in consequence of
the non arrival of some articles that were expected from Lisbon." He thought
they would be there any day, and he hoped they would not have to linger here
much longer:

> I see by the General orders they are busy making fascines with the army
> supposed to be preparatory to the siege, but I should think it can be noth-
> ing but a feint.

In fact, Wellington was carrying out more than a feint; he was close to
starting his siege of Ciudad Rodrigo. Fascines were large rectangles made of
woven wicker that were used to line the trenches, to strengthen the walls:

> I suppose all hopes of my getting a Co. for these 2 or 3 years are now at
> an end, at least I have given them up so that should it happen sooner I
> shall at any rate have the pleasure of being aggreeably disappointed. I
> shall not expect it much as long as I retain the command of such a Co. as
> I have at present.[3]

"This would be a very pleasant quarters were it not for the very wet
weather which endures." The streets, however, were excessively filthy so that
going out was disagreeable. Throughout Portugal, people dumped their slops
into the street below. The narrower the street the more malodorous the place.
When Francis reported that a town or city was filthy, he probably was referring
to the stench. He had not complained of filth in London, for at the time the city
had a rudimentary sewerage system. Granted, the pipes led to the Thames,
which turned the river itself into a sewer, but the farther from the water the better the air smelt.

Coimbra was a very rich city, and was recovering from ravages wrought
during the retreat from Bussaco. The Convent of Santa Cruz, he found excessively fine, and the gardens attached to it beautiful beyond description and so
extensive that one would need two or three days to view them properly. The

The Library, University of Coimbra. This may have been the library Francis so admired.

walks were laid out with a great deal of taste, and the numerous fountains and temples were also very beautiful:

> The orange groves are at present laden with fruit which add much to the beauty. There are likewise some very curious chrisanthamums. The rectory where the Friars dine is a very fine room & they live in a very sumptuous style. At the head of the room are figures as large as life of the 12 apostles sitting down for passover. The figures are well executed.

The kitchen was downright ornate. He admired several fountains right in the room, and there were galeries nearly 200 feet long above him in which were many paintings. His mouth watered at the sight of the fish, flesh and fowl that were about to be cooked. He thought the luxury would astonish any observer. He was still a hungry fellow, always ready for a meal, and after so long on the army food, which was ample but boring, he was predisposed to enjoy Coimbra, and to spend a bit more than Elizabeth would have approved.

He had found a "tolerably good" museum, and a very fine library. The buildings in the town were superb, the finest he had seen anywhere in Portugal, and that included Lisbon:

> I saw a very handsome procession the other day in the university and a man ordained as Doctor of Religion with which I was much pleased. There are numberless convents in this town. They are mostly all the same sort but this one [the one he visited that had the fine kitchen] is superior to any I have found in Portugal.

Coimbra, very beautiful, was situated on the banks of the Mondego River, and built into the decline of the hill, as was the case with a number of towns he had seen. The environs were also beautiful and in some places "very wide & romantic." He estimated that the town was not much more than half the size of Lisbon:

> It was a very happy thing for Portugal that the French could not make their retreat through this town as it is one of the richest & best towns in Portugal, and I think would have injured the country [with] as much damage as almost all the other towns that they destroyed.[4]

He referred to Masséna's retreat following his stay outside the Lines of Torres Vedras, not his pursuit of the allied army after the Battle of Bussaco. Apparently he bypassed Coimbra, although it was in direct line with Almeida.

Before the 27th Regiment marched from Celorico, Francis learned that the 4th Division would have a temporary change of commander. General Lowry Cole had taken a leave of absence and was going home. His wound had healed satisfactorily, but he was a Member of Parliament and he wanted to take his seat for a while. His replacement was Major General Charles Coville, who had commanded a brigade in Picton's 3rd Division. Francis thought he would be a fine commanding officer. He had been Picton's right hand man and was much respected by Lord Wellington.

His Lordship had been improving his communications by use of naval "telegraphs", the system of raising and lowering verticle rows of bladders by means of light cords strung from pulleys on the bottom to more pulleys attached to a high cross beam. They could spell out signals according to the number of bladders hoisted on any one cord. To operate them, young midshipmen were detached from their ships to serve at points from which the telegraph could be seen for a good distance, especially by officers with telescopes. The other improvement was in the quantity of heavy guns he was able to assemble around Elvas. Guns that gathered at Sebutal, at the mouth of the Sado River below Lisbon, moved part way by boat, but more by road through defiles and over high hills – 18 and 24 pounders.

The siege train would consist of fifty-two guns, under the command of Captain Alexander Dickson of the Royal Artillery. To help with the trenching and other construction, Wellington had again asked Prme Minister Lord Liverpool for trained sappers and miners, but none had come. Fortunately, he received 115 men of the Royal Military Artificers, and his troops had become more skilled at digging trenches, work they loathed.[5] Francis' Grenadier company would be doing its full share, digging, or guarding the working parties.

Meanwhile, back home at Wolford Lodge, Elizabeth and his sisters were proudly reading a most gratifying letter in praise of Francis from an old friend of John Graves Simcoe. The sender was George Mackenzie, probably a relation of Major General Alexander Mackenze, Francis' first brigade commander. George Mackenzie had recently seen Colonel John Maclean, battalion commander of the 27th Regiment.

Mackenzie was ready to do the smallest kindness for the son of a man whose memory "will ever be most affectionately and respectfully cherished by me." He felt that Mrs. Simcoe had done him justice in assuming that he retained an interest in the family of Simcoe:

> I am more than pleased it should so happen, that I can make this letter highly acceptable to you as a Mother, and to your daughters who will be with you, feel an honest pride in having the unsought praises of your eldest Son

> I have lately had the pleasure of his commanding Officer, Coll. McLean, who is just returned from Portugal. The very warm eulogisms he gave your son, quite delighted me. He spoke of him as one of the best young officers he had ever known, of his conduct and disposition he expressed

himself in terms equally satisfactory and in short it has never happened to me before to hear a more pleasing account of a young man.

I feel it necessary to add that Coll. McLean is a most excellent officer and a good judge of Military merit, and I assure you his testimony in favour of Mr. Simcoe is the more valuable as he is not, in general, a man of many words nor one who would sing the praises of any one, merely to please. I was very glad to hear from Coll. McLean that your son is so near getting a company, he said he should try everything in his power to get him back into the 27th Regt.

He apologized for the length of his letter, but because the subject was of no small interest, he could not deny himself the pleasure of forwarding to the family what he considered strictly as honest and honourable praise.[6] He closed with, "My Father desires me to offer you his most respectful regards. My sisters are on a visit to [friends] at Bath. I beg my compliments to the Misses Simcoe ..."

This letter confirms other strong evidence that pointed to Francis as one of the finest junior officers – the dinner as Wellington's guest, the support of Lord Moira, and now his own battalion commander, Lieutenant Colonel Maclean. He had had good reports from everyone who worked with him, but Horse Guards, at Whitehall, could not be moved. Rules were rules. Lieutenant Simcoe did not have the seniority for promotion.

If Francis could lead a forlorn hope somewhere, and survive, that would alter the prospect. While he was idling in Coimbra, owing to the slowness of the arrival of the equipment and clothing the 27th Regiment needed, Wellington's army was in action against Ciudad Rodrigo. By mid January heavy guns drawn from Almeida had been set in emplacements, and were opening up two wide breaches in walls of Ciudad Rodrigo. Two lieutenants had received permission to lead forlorn hopes to each opening. Each lieutenant might command up to fifty volunteers who would rush into the breaches, under cover of guns firing grape and cannister shot at the defenders, fired high enough to avoid hitting the small assaulting parties. Then the guns would stop as the men climbed higher and, swords drawn and bayonets fixed, pray the mad rush would succeed. Behind them would follow about 500 more volunteers, and if they were not wiped out, the army would press forward in a mass to overwhelm the defenders. The defenders, of course, had the edge, sheltered behind walls while the attackers had little cover and paid a price.

The two chosen lieutenants were John Gurwood and William Pearce. Gurwood, who survived a severe skull wound, became famous as the editor of Wellington's dispatches. More important, shortly after Ciudad Rodrigo he was promoted captain in the Royal African corps, not a very prestigious regiment, but he soon exchanged into the 9th Light Dragoons.[7] Lieutenant Pearce, who was killed in the breach, had caught Wellington's attention owing to a brawl in a brothel. His court martial acquitted him honourably. Wellington ordered "honourably" deleted because performing in a brothel had no honour.[8] The brawl had occurred at Coimbra, in October 1809, during the withdrawal from Bussaco towards the Lines of Torres Vedras.

Francis listened to the reports of the successful storming and capture of Ciudad Rodrigo in envious silence. He heard that Colonel John Colborne, hit in the arm, had led 450 volunteers in the capture of the main outwork that overlooked the town's defenses. For weeks beforehand, the troops had been trenching, as usual with inferior tools. With fragile, dull blades they had had to hack at the snow-covered ground, guarded by some of Rowland Hill's division. The allied army was 35,000 strong; the garrison inside Ciudad Rodrigo 2,000 men. Marmont had withdrawn to Salamanca. Wellington was anxious to strike before Marmont could relieve the fortress. He planned to have Thomas Picton's 3rd Division storm the main larger breach on the right, while Robert Crawford took his Light Division into the smaller one on the left.

On the left, Gurwood led his forlorn hope, of twenty-five, followed by the storming party under Captain George Napier, of 300 men of the 52nd Regiment. Gurwood, Napier and Crauford were all wounded. Napier lost an arm, but Crauford's wound was mortal. The loss of Crauford shocked everyone from Wellington down. On the right, Picton's 3rd Division's Colonel Daniel Mackinnon and his Connaught Rangers spearheaded the strong attack with a bayonet charge. Mackinnon was killed when a mine exploded. Wellington had 200 killed and 700 wounded. The French lost 300 in killed and wounded, and 1,500 were taken prisoner. In June-July 1810, the French, under Marshal Michel Ney, had required twenty-five days to capture the fortressed town. Once the preliminary trenching had been completed, Wellington's army retook it in just two days of bombardment.

When the battalions had come streaming into the town through the gates, the troops ran wild. Picton and other officers tried to establish order, but failed entirely. After the hard work in the trenches, the strain of the campaign, and the loss of some comrades through French resistance, the men were in no mood to return quietly to their encampments. They wanted revenge, not just for this battle, but for all the earlier ones, and they took it. They looted houses, shops, particularly wine shops, and removed everything of value they could find. Their behaviour was disgraceful, but understandable. Deserters who had gone over to the French were imprisoned, and some would soon face execution. Wellington's immediate concern was not the looting but the care of the wounded. By that time Francis and the 27th Regiment had started back along the Mondego River, his battalion with decent clothes, boots or shoes, and most of the worn out equipment had been repaired or renewed.

Already Wellington's plans for the attack on the last fortress standing between Portugal and Spain were well advanced. First, he wanted to get his guns moving towards Elvas. The brass toys would be remounted to ornament that fortress' walls. He wanted to show a large army along the border with the Spanish Province of Leon, opposite northern Portugal as long as possible, to convince Marmont that he was not going to the Esdremadura, south of Leon. He kept his headquarters at Freneda, near Fuentes de Onoro, but he had sent the three brigades of Rowland Hill's 2nd Division to Castello Branco at the beginning of January, where they were stationed during the siege of Cuidad Rodrigo. The other divisions would be moving before the beginning of March.

By 1 February, the 27th Regiment had returned to Almeida, and were accommodated at a village Francis called Villa de Agua. He had been to Ciudad Rodrigo, and had "examined the place very minutely." It was a very old fortification, surrounded by a single wall which at first appearance seemed to be not very strong. It was composed of small pebbles instead of larger stones generally used in building fortifications, but it had stood for considerable battering from Wellington's guns. Ciudad Rodrigo was pleasantly situated on the Spanish side of the banks of the Agueda River, with a handsome bridge over the water and commanded on one side by a hill. There had been a lot of rain of late, and the Agueda was no longer fordable. "We are all going into regular cantonments shortly and it is supposed we shall move towards the Alemtejo [Alentego] in the spring. " Elvas would be used as the base from which to launch yet another attempt on Badajoz:

> I have received a long letter from Pring, and am sorry to find him so far from being recovered contrary to what I had a right to expect from an account we heard of but a short time before. I am anxiously expecting a packet daily. You heard in my last [letter] of my being superceded in the command of the Gr. Co.[9]

The axe had fallen. He tried to sustain some hope of a company, although it could never be the one he wanted most. Perhaps in two or three months, when he had more time to attend to the regiment, Lord Moira might still use his influence. In fact, Moira did not have time; he was preoccupied with his own plans because he would shortly be appointed governor general of Bengal and commander in chief in India.

For the time being, Francis tried to reconcile himself to becoming as useful as possible to the new captain of the Grenadier Company whenever he arrived – to obey again before he could command.

Chapter 19
The Costly Third Siege, 6 April 1812

Francis found his brother officers sympathetic, but there was little they could say. The other captains had had no objection to a promotion of so young a lad because he was capable and had their trust. The men of the Grenadier Company were quietly disappointed. Some were twice his age, but they would have followed him anywhere. Horse Guards was all powerful. Even Wellington could not have his way. Colonel Maclean, very sorry for Francis, reminded him that their chief could not rid himself of Sir William Erskine, who was undoubtedly insane. Wellington had sent him home in 1809, but Horse Guards returned him a year later. Erskine was the officer who had allowed the French garrison to escape from Almeida. Francis never named his new captain, and never mentioned him in his letters to Elizabeth or his sisters. Grandfather Simcoe's maxims helped. If his turn did not come soon, Wellington would need at least one forlorn hope any day now. If Lieutenant Gurwood could survive, so could Lieutenant Simcoe.

"Badajoz" was upon everyone's lips. Wellington had deceived Marmont by remaining so long at Freneda, but his divisions were on the move. When he returned from Coimbra, Francis located the 4th Division inside Spain, at San Felices, twenty miles north of Ciudad Rodrigo, and five miles east of the Alguera River, and at Sesmiro, an even tinier village nearby.[1]

The 7th Division had passed through Castelo Branco on 26 February, the 6th Division on the 29th, the Light Division on 3 March, and the 4th Division on the 5th, the day Wellngton set out from Freneda. All went through Portalegre, Vila Vicosa or Castello de Vide, and were in touch with Elvas by 8 March. The 1st Division, coming from Abrantes where they had received new clothing, joined on 10 March. Two Portuguese divisions went by circuitous routes, one through Coimbra, the other by Tomar, and did not arrive near Elvas until he 16th. The 5th Division did not leave Ciudad Rodrigo until 9 March.[2] Thus while Marmont remained convinced that the bulk of the army was still in the north, Wellington was able to assemble the army he was sending against Badajoz to places within easy reach of Elvas.

The troops who remained behind were chiefly Portuguese militia and 15,000 men of four weak Spanish divisions. With them remained the King's German Legion, who could be relied upon not to turn tail if Marmont appeared.

At Elvas, Rowland Hill's 2nd Division was already encamped. Although the cavalrymen of the King's German Legion were at Ciudad Rodrigo, a brigade of German heavy dragoons that had landed recently at Lisbon had ridden to Elvas, to reinforce a British brigade. Now Wellington had two brigades to pit against Soult's powerful horsemen. Two Portuguese brigades were on hand, but they were light dragoons.

When Wellington arrived on 12 May, siege material was already parked on the glacis (slopes) of Elvas. Fifty-two guns had arrived, with 300 British and 560 Portuguese artillerymen to slave over loading, priming, firing and swabbing out two extinguish sparks before any could ignite before loading the next shot. Wellington had had a quarrel with Admiral Berkeley, who had been so kind to Francis in Lisbon. Berkeley refused to detach twenty 18-pounder ship guns from the *Barfleur*. Instead he offered twenty Russian guns that were a different calibre and would not fit the round shot used in British-made cannons. Captain Alexander Dickson had scrounged around Lisbon and found some ammunition that would fit, and, Wellington, furious with Berkeley, had to be satisfied.[3] On hand were twenty-two pontoons, enough to bridge the 300-yard wide Guardiana. Stacked about were fascines and gabions Some of the latter were cylinders of metal, that could be filled with earth to strengthen trench walls.

For the allies the most serious weakness remained the engineers, the want of sappers and miners. The 115 military artificers were too few. Again men from the line regiments had to perform as sappers. Wellington lamented that every French Corps had one battalion of sappers and one company of miners. For this defect the allied army would pay dearly in lives. Ciudad Rodrigo had been relatively easy, even with the poor tools. Badajoz presented a far more formidable challenge.

The walls were still thirty feet high, the eight bastions again staring menacingly towards the encampment. Inside was a garrison more than twice the size of Ciudad Rodrigo, and under a very capable governor, General Armand Philippon, who had made the best preparations he could to impede entry into the town. As well, inside were many Spanish residents sympathetic to the French (a guarantee that a sacking of Badajoz would make Ciudad Rodrigo seem almost friendly).

General Philippon had strengthened his bastions and the three most important outlying forts, Picurina on the east side of the Rivillas River; Pardaleras to the south; and San Cristobal, across the Guardiana, the scene of the vicious fight of the first siege that had made Francis acting captain. The glacis and counterscarp had been raised at San Cristobal and a strong redoubt,

Lunette Werlé (named for a general who had fallen at Albuera) faced north. The French had thrown old pieces of metal, sharp rocks, old carts, rotten boats, broken gabions and fascines and anything they could think of to make the ditches killing fields. If Wellington succeeded in opening breaches, Philippon had obstacles piled high to throw into them. His troops had dammed up the

Modern view of Badajoz, showing the Guardiana River, the bridge that led to the Tête de Pont Fort, and the ochre walls of the town and castle.

Rivillas River just below the San Roque Lunette, and turned the water along the east side of Badajoz into a huge shallow lake right up to the town wall.

Philippon's garrison, 4,700 strong, consisted of five battalions of French regulars, 2,767 men, two battalions of the Hesse-Darmstadt Regiment, 910 men, three companies of artillery, 261 men, two and one half companies of sappers, 260 men, 42 cavalrymen, a company of Spanish *Juramentados,* and the escort of a convoy that had reached the town two days before Wellington began the siege. Provisions were adequate but not plentiful.[4]

The other obstacle was the weather. Rain poured down day after day, filling the trenches with water and deepening the lake created by the dam on the Rivillas. During a severe storm the pontoon bridge broke loose and sailed sweeping down the Guardiana.

Francis' first letter from Badajoz to Elizabeth was dated 21 March, in which he described the digging, and a famous sortie the French made towards the British trenches:

> We invested this town with the 3rd & 4th and Light Divisions on the 11th of this month & took ground on the 17th, a most tremendous stormy night, but notwithstanding there was a great deal of work done & we lost no men from the darkness of the night. On the 20th there was a good deal of work done, the weather still stormy, our losses minimal. On the 19th the enemy made a sortie. They entered our trenches & did no further damage than taking away a few entrenching tools. They were repulsed with considerable loss, it is thought to have amounted to 20 killed & 200 wounded. ... [the brunt fell upon] our Regiment, we lost upwards of 30 men.[5]

During the sortie, Colonel Richard Fletcher, the commanding engineer, had been wounded. Junior officers had to carry on without him. The parties of troops finished their works on the 20th, 21st and 22nd, and believed they were ready to open the bombardment, although the weather continued unfavourable:

> Our duty was excessively hard, having scarcely a night in bed, furnishing near 4000 men at a time for working & fatigue parties. 23rd, the batteries would have opened but constant rain had undone a great deal of our work. On the 24th all got ready & on the 25th our artillery opened [fire] with considerble effect.

Wellington decided that the Picurina Fort must be taken first. In British hands, guns could be brought within range to hurdle round shot (cannon balls) against the two bastions that faced it – Trinidad and Santa Maria. After guns already mounted in batteries to the east had bombarded Picurina and silenced its guns, he assigned Major General James Kempt and 500 men of the Light and 3rd Divisions to attack. They stormed the small fort at ten o'clock at night, expecting the ditch to be filled with rubbish. The defenders had cleaned it out, deepening it considerably. Only the salient angle of the scarp had been damaged by the guns. The French kept up a brisk musket fire, and 100 men had been struck down before they reached the ditch.

Two small flanking columns tried to get in through a ravine that carried a small tributary of the Rivillas, but found the way blocked by a double row of palisades. They found a place that was narrower, and sent men for thirty-foot scaling ladders. These would reach across the narrow spot. The ladders sagged dangerously but held, and about fifty men of the 88th Connaught Rangers obtained a foothold at the salient, the only damaged spot, and broke inside. After a stubborn resistance, the governor, Colonel Gaspard-Thierry, surrendered. Kempt took 145 prisoners, but one officer and forty men managed to escape into Badajoz. Kempt had lost more than half his force. Philippon made

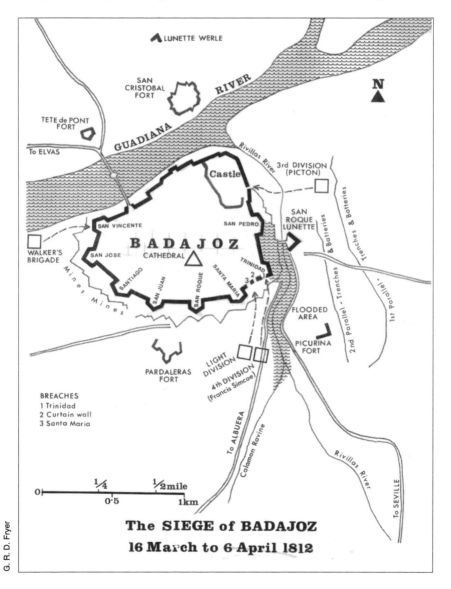

The SIEGE of BADAJOZ
16 March to 6 April 1812

G. R. D. Fryer

a sortie from the San Roque Lunette, but was driven back losing fifty in killed and wounded.

Francis' perspective was less detached:

> Last night (the 25th) Fort Picurina, a small fort near the town & occupied by the enemy, was taken by storm. We carried it, & the Enemy attempted to retake it with 500 men but were repulsed with considerable loss. It is supposed near 200 men were bayonetted in the fort & 70 or 80 made prisoners. Our loss for the whole less than 200 killed & wounded, it was considered very dashing and was absolutely necessary for the carrying of our works.[6]

Five pieces of artillery were taken. The 5th Division, that had set out last, had arrived and was operating on the Portuguese side of the Guardiana River. Hill's 2nd Division was forward, keeping watch in the direction of Talavera in case Marmont should be moving from that neighbourhood. The 3rd Division was on the Spanish side. Francis had written as accurate an account as circumstances would allow, and he had been able to see a lot from the line of trenches the army had built along the east bank of the Rivillas. His battalion had been working there, but he wrote his description from a hut that barely kept out the worst of the hammering rain. "I am going in a few minutes to the trenches which is an excuse for my taking leave of you... The [French] garrison consists of 4000 men & is supposed Marmont & Soult will not be able to relieve the town, everything is carried on with such rapidity & success".

The trenches lay parallel to the Rivillas River, along a slight incline. Here was the line they called the first parallel. Under the direction of the artillery officers the men were erecting a row of gun batteries. They had seven batteries, but these were too far off to endanger the walls of Badajoz. Now that Kempt had taken Picurina Fort, the troops were able to start work on a second, inner parallel of trenches, and to erect two batteries within range. San Cristobal was very strong, but Pardaleros could be isolated. Wellington thought that if he could take Badajoz first, San Cristobal would not likely try to hold out.

Back in Devonshire, on 28 March the Simcoes' accountant, Mr. Christopher Flood, had made one more appeal to Horse Guards. On 31 March, he received a reply. The writer (the signature is illegible) could not possibly comply with Mr. Flood's request, no matter how willing he was to oblige him. Obtaining a step of promotion was a matter of such extreme difficulty that he had no possible means within his reach of affording the least assistance. The regulated difference between a lieutenancy and a company was £950, and there was no possibility of purchasing the captaincy by giving more money than the regulated value.

The writer referred to a corrupt practice that the Duke of York had stopped, a bidding game for commissions. Formerly some men had succeeded in gaining a commission by bribing the vendor with the offer of a far higher price than the official one. Even that unfair custom no longer existed. An officer was no longer permitted to find his own buyers, but now "no step of promotion whatever is allowed to go otherwise than by the nomination of the Commander in Chief, in consequence of which shall be within compass when I tell you there are not less than 200 Lieutenants whose names are before the Commander in Chief".

By "Commander in Chief" the writer did not mean Wellington. He meant the Duke of York, now reinstated after the disgrace caused by his mistress. The writer then stated the case against "purchasing a promotion outside the Regiment". It was very rare, he explained, for a company to be sold out of a regiment, which meant purchasing a promotion from one regiment to another. Where one man might succeed, many more must be disappointed:

> This is to be regretted that in turning to the Army List I perceive a great many Lieuts. above Lieut. Simcoe in the 27th which gives him but a very distant hope of Promotion in the Regt. He should however not omit to return his name as a Purchaser at Head Quarters in case a vacancy should occur and the Lieuts above him decline. In addition to that there is nothing to be done but to exert all the Interest that can be made with the Commander in Chief, as it is only by that means that he can succeed otherwise than as it may come to his turn in the the the Regt.[7]

The letter was written only a week before the storming of Badajoz. Had Francis known, he would have been driven to seek permission to lead a forlorn hope. Like John Gurwood, his promotion to captain would have been automatic.

The capture of the Picurina Fort was the beginning of the end for the French garrison inside Badajoz. Picurina stood on a commanding knoll, a mere 400 yards from the Trinidad Bastion, and 450 from the Santa Maria. From 26 to 30 March, the men were employed establishing batteries. All the time the men were working the French fired a hail of projectiles among them. They erected two batteries at Picurina, as part of a second parallel of trenches. Of the other bastions, commencing at the castle on its hilltop and moving south, then west and north to the bridge to Tête de Pont Fort, the eight bastions were:

San Pedro, covering the San Roque Lunette, the Trinidad, Santa Maria, San Roque, San Juan, Santiago, San José, and San Vincente.

Partisans who spied for Wellington reported a row of mines from Santiago to San José zone to be avoided. Now that the allies controlled Picurina, the best targets were Trinidad and Santa Maria, and there the bombardment began. Meanwhile, they tried to do something about the inundation on the Rivillas. As long as the water remained here, breaches, once they were practicable, could only be reached by a narrow, vulnerable route between the water's edge and the steep slope of the Pardaleras Fort. Wellington intended to launch his assault from the trenches, but that would be costly unless the Rivillas had fallen to its natural level. All the artillery fire sent towards the dam had failed. Someone would have to blow it up.

The task fell to a lieutenant of engineers and twenty sappers, the latter surely all the army had. On the night of 2 April, the party, all the while under French fire, slipped down a ravine and laid bags of black powder against the dam. The powder exploded, but it merely injured the dam. On the 3rd they attempted to sap (trench) down to the dam but so many were killed at the head of the sap and the zig-zags advanced so slowly that the effort was abandoned. The assaults on the breaches would have to be launched only from the the the Rivillas side.

The two breaches were widening, the larger at Trinidad, the smaller in Santa Maria, while a third spot, between them, was crumbling. The efforts of the French to heal them and impede the allies were valiant. The allies tried to fill the ditches below the breaches with the debris the guns were creating, but French troops would be sent out at night to empty them while guns fired grape shot over their heads to keep the allied troops at a distance.[8] It seemed to Francis and his brother officers that whenever the artillerymen damaged a French gun and put it out of action, Philippon merely substituted another. Apparently the French had an unlimited supply of guns. By 4 April French fire was slackening, because they were running low on ammunition. Wellington moved forward a dozen siege guns he had reserved to use at three supplementary batteries, numbers 10, 11 and 12. By the 4th the breaches were becoming "practicable."

A message arrived that Soult had crossed the Sierra Morena with a substantial army. Marmont, fortunately, had gone raiding into central Portugal on an order from Napoleon himself. If Soult got too close to Badajoz, Wellington would have to detach some troops to join the covering force he had already sent to watch for him. Nosey was not worried about Marmont, who would not be able to make a junction with Soult, but he could not afford to let Soult get much nearer before he made his assault. By the 5th the breaches were practicable, but the wounded Colonel Fletcher, who was barely fit for duty, was alarmed that the French were building an inner wall between the houses inside Badajoz that would form another line of defence once the troops entered the town. Success at the breaches might still mean failure afterwards.

Wellington felt he could not afford to listen to Fletcher. He would storm the breaches on the night of 6 April, Easter Monday. On Sunday the chaplains could prepare special services of celebration of the Ressurection and thanksgiving to comfort and reassure the men.

His Lordship decided that the 4th Division, led by Charles Colville, would assault the Trinidad breach. The 3,500 men would have to move closest to the water, a narrow, cramped approach. An advance party of 500 would follow the forlorn hope, carrying twelve siege ladders, and bags of hay to drop into the ditches to help break the men's fall. The Light Division would attack the breach in the flank wall of the Santa Maria.[9] Meanwhile, Thomas Picton's 3rd Division would march along the east bank of the Rivillas until they were well downstream of the dam and out of range of guns at San Roque Lunette. There they would cross to the west bank and try to gain access to the castle. James Leith's 5th Division would attempt to break through on the left of the San Vincente bastion, where the French had not placed mines.

The Light and 4th Divisions would march in column from their trenches behind Picurina Fort, cross the ravine to the east of the road to Albuera, and when close enough to the breaches, the 4th would swing right towards Trinidad, and the Light to the left towards Santa Maria. The main thrust would be on the breaches; Picton's and Leith's were to serve as diversions, taking some pressure off the 4th and Light Divisions, and if possible succeeding in their own missions.

Easter Sunday was one of subdued reverence. The divisions marched to their church parades, but most of the day passed in checking equipment. Flints had to be screwed down properly, or if the flint was too worn, it was replaced. Bayonets were sharpened and gleaming, cartridge cases full. Francis anticipated that they would charge the breach with the bayonet alone, but opportunities to load and fire might arise. In the evening he had a long talk with the Reverend George Jenkins, which had a calming effect.

The chaplain raised the matter of a will, but Francis pretended not to hear, and quickly put it out of his mind. He was not going to die; none of the men were. Any man who faced what Wellington's army faced would surely not survive if he went in expecting to be killed. No. A man had to be positive, and to anticipate only the thrill of marching into the captured town, colours flying.

The French had not been idle. More impediments had landed in the ditches. On the slopes they had laid doors through which long spikes had been driven; among them were caltrops (four-spiked iron balls). Once the assaults started a chevaux de frise, of Spanish cavalry swords, the handles firmly fastened to a wooden beam, would be hung across each breach, firmly anchored lethal points facing the attackers.

Wellington had chosen half past seven in the twilight for the assault to commence, but it did not begin until ten o'clock. All columns were ordered to strike at the same time, which meant careful coordination. By the appointed time, some of the various parts were not ready. Even the ten o'clock starting time was uneven. Picton's men had been fired upon fifteen minutes before the cathedral clock struck ten. The leader of the advance party carrying ladders and hay bags lost his way before he could give leadership and Leith's men did not start until eleven. Only the Light and 4th Divisions began their assaults at the ordered time. John Harvey's Portuguese brigade came next. Kemmis' brigade, of the 3rd Battalion 27th and the 1st Battalion 40th Regiment, brought up the rear. The Portuguese were courageous, but they would be steadied by the fusiliers in front and the two regiments behind.

The 4th Division advanced, found itself blocked by the flooded Rivillas and was forced to move to the left into the zone the Light Division was supposed to occupy. The two divisions became intermingled. Of the 500 in the storming party of the 4th, nearly all were killed or severely wounded. Water in the ditches was so deep that some men drowned. The French kept up a steady musket fire from the walls; their remaining stocks of grape and canister shot rained down from the undamaged parts of the bastions. Kemmis' brigade had come to a halt, unable to proceed when everything in front was stalled. Some men climbed upon a partly built ravelin (detached, outwork) but instead of being able to continue towards the breach they faced a steep drop with no way down and had to turn back.

The brigade advanced when the way seemed to clear, mainly because so many men of the two brigades ahead of them were lying in the ditch while their comrades climbed over them. Somewhere in the melee Lieutenant Francis Simcoe drew his sabre, called to followers, and began forcing his way towards the broken wall.

Chapter 20

A Warrior Taking His Rest

On 9 April, Chaplain George Jenkins of the 4th Division wrote to Mrs. Simcoe:

The perfectly unknown, yet my feelings dictate that I shd. in the present melancholy reason address you, as I am aware yr. anxiety must be respecting the fate of my most esteemed friend, you Son, sincerely lamented by all who knew him, he fell on the night of the 6th in the midst of several others his Brother Officers & hundreds of his fellow Country men while storming the town of Badajos [sic]. To state the details of this circumstance wd. be needless. In him I have lost a promising young friend, an agreeable companion, & good Christian, & allow me most sincerely to sympathise & condole with you in the gt. loss you have sustained by the death of an affect. & dutiful Son.

On the morning of the 7th, I went in search of my esteemed & valued young friend, & was fortunate to find him lying in the breach. When (as I am sure it will be satisfactory for a friend & Parent to be informed) I performed the last offices over him & got him as decently interred as the gt. confusion of our most melancholy situation wd. admit. He has left no memorandum behind him, tho frequently intreated by me in case of accidents, neither did he make any requests when I parted with him, but committed his fate entirely to Him who is the Deposer of all events. Proffering to you & yr. afflicted family my future services in any way I can be useful, allow me to subscribe &c, George Jenkins, Chaplain to the forces 4th Div. Badajos Camp, April 9th, 1812.[1]

Of some 15,000 troops sent to assault Badajoz, fully a third were casualties. British losses were 806 officers and men killed, and 2,310 officers and men wounded. The Portuguese lost 155 officers and men killed, and 545 officers and men wounded with 30 missing.[2] When Wellington inspected the breaches on the morning of 7 April, he could not control his own tears. Officers who saw him recalled the aftermath of Badajoz as the only time they had seen their chief weep.

The first assault on the breaches at ten o'clock on the night of 6 April had lasted until midnight, The men refused to admit defeat until Wellington, waiting on a hill above the second parallel, sent orders for the recall of the Light and 4th Divisions. The appalling carnage had only one positive effect. The slaughter at the breaches distracted the French from the work of the 3rd and 5th divisions. General Thomas Picton's 3rd faced a rugged climb up a cliff which the previous generation would have compared to the climb of General James Wolfe's soldiers to the Plains of Abraham in 1759.

Picton had been studying the wall and cliff, noting low spots in both and directing men towards them. Even after reaching the top of the cliff, the men had to put the scaling ladders they had dragged up with them against the thirty-foot high wall. Ladder after ladder was thrown back, hurling most of the men who had succeeded in climbing on them to their deaths. With the assaults on the breaches proving a near disaster, Wellington sent an urgent message to General Picton to be determined to reach the castle. Picton was hit in the groin, and his second in command, James Kempt, took charge of the division. Kempt's brigade made the first rush, followed by the Portuguese. Both were stopped. The brigade under Major General T. Campbell reached them. Now 4,000 men were arrayed at the base of the wall, a front about 200 yards wide. At last, sheer volume overwhelmed the defenders.[3]

The detachment in the castle was small, under 300 men. Finally so many attackers were at the top that some were bound to get inside. Many more men came up the ladders safely, until the garrison had to withdraw into the streets, and the 3rd Division was soon flocking after the French. Picton was again on the scene; Kempt had been wounded, more seriously than Picton, who forced himself to limp back up the slope to the wall. Some of the enemy in the castle put up stiff resistance, seeking the protection of the keep and firing at Picton's men, but they were so outnumbered that the situation was hopeless.

The French at the breaches had to detach some of the defenders to deal with the threat from the rear. In the meantime Walker's brigade in Leith's 5th Division were attacking the San Vincente bastion, amidst firing from it, and the San José. The thirty foot wall presented the same difficulties as faced Picton's men and those at the breaches. Officers scouting found a spot on the flank where the wall was only twenty feet high. They ordered scaling ladders, and the men were soon pouring in. The San Vincente, too, had only a small garrison. Several companies had been sent to the breaches. Leith's men also captured the San José bastion, but they met with very stiff resistance at the Santiago. Capturing it was not important; they had done enough.

When the battered Light and 4th Divisions made their second assault, they succeeded. The numerical weakness of French garrison showed up when they had to battle on three fronts. Wellington knew he had won. He received an added bonus when men left to guard the trenches poured out, captured the isolated San Roque Lunette, and broke open the dam on the Rivillas. The minor event was gratifying but Badajoz was already Wellington's.

Immediately graves had to be found for some 1,200 bodies. One solution was mass burials. Francis Simcoe was luckier than many because of the con-

Wolford Chapel on a rainy May day, the Ontario flag flying. The chapel is now the property of the people of Ontario.

cern the Reverend George Jenkins had shown for his remains. Reports on his end were brief, merely that he had died in the breach at Badajoz. He was in the attack on the Trinidad breach, surely the most dangerous place to be. The fact that the chaplain had been able to find his body suggests that he might have survived the first assault and fallen at the second. Just where he was will likely remain a mystery, because he did not live long enough to fulfil the promise of his early career. He was cut down before his achievements could justify inclusion in the *Dictionary of National Biography* – ahead of the account about his father. John Gurwood merited recognition in the dictionary because of his later successes.

Three possibilities on Francis' exact role present themselves. The first is that he did lead a forlorn hope. He was certainly desperate enough to ask Major General Kemmis to recommend him to General Colville. If he had done so, and been refused a forlorn hope, the reason could have been his widowed mother, who might be left with only one, much younger, surviving son. The second possibility is that he was commanding a platoon, half a company, while the new captain led the other half of the Grenadiers of the 27th Regiment. The third, no less improbable, is that the new captain had not yet arrived in the Peninsula. Such delays were far from unusual in the British army of Wellngton's time. In the absence of the captain, Francis would have commanded the Grenadier Company himself.

The new captain, whom Francis never named, was probably Francis Bignall, whose commission was dated 14 November 1811. The date of the commission of the next captain, shown on The Army List for 1813, was 6 February 1812, too late. Francis knew he had been superceded by 1 February.

When the chaplain's letter reached Wolford Lodge, a pall of sadness descended, and not only over Elizabeth, Francis' sisters and twelve-year-old Henry. As soon as he was informed, Lord Moira wrote a letter of condolence:

> Whether a letter my dear Madam might not be an intrusion upon your powers is a consideration which has been perplexing me. Still, I can not fear the possibility of your doubting what I feel upon this calamitous event. The loss appears to me not less mine than yours.[4]

He had grown fond of "our young soldier" during the month he had spent in Francis' company before he left for Ireland. He had followed reports on him, gratified at how favourable they had been. He well knew the risks of war, but mixed with his own regrets was guilt that he had lost the son of a valued comrade.

Miss Mary Anne Burges was devastated. The young man she loved as a son was no more. The hopes she had cherished of a union between Francis and Julia died with him. How the Hon. Julia Somerville felt about Francis is another mystery. They were certainly good friends. Julia had been raised as another sister. The request Francis made that he should give her the topaz ring was no small matter. A young gentleman did not offer jewellery to a young lady unless he felt more than friendship for her.

(Four years later, in 1816, Julia married her first cousin once removed, Francis Bond Head, the 6th lieutenant governor of Upper Canada. She was a witness to the Rebellion of 1837, which her husband did little to avoid and much to promote.)

After she lost her dear Francis, Elizabeth Simcoe decided that enough men in her life had been sacrificed to the military. She had been denied even knowing her own father. Her husband had died far too young, because of strenuous service to the public. Now Francis lay buried in the Trinidad breach in faraway Spain. John Graves Simcoe reposed in the family cemetery beside Wolford Chapel, but Elizabeth's father, Thomas Gwillim, like her eldest son,

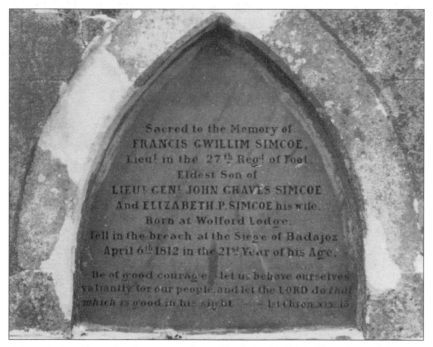

Memorial to Francis Simcoe on the wall of the Wolford Chapel.

lay buried near a battlefield. Henry Addington Simcoe, Elizabeth resolved, would be for the church. Henry's name, not Francis', precedes their father's in the *Dictionary of National Biography*.

The Peninsular War continued, with Wellington's successes at Salamanca, his entry into Madrid, and in 1813 Vitoria, by which time a corps of Royal Sappers and Miners was being formed, as Wellington had long requested.

Wellington kept moving forward until the allies entered Paris in March 1814. Napoleon abdicated on 6 April, exactly two years after Badajoz. The entire Peninsular War had been a ghastly bloodbath, and one that never should have occurred. In attacking Spain, Napoleon was asking for failure. The Peninsula did not provide enough food for an army living off the country, and France could only trickle provisions through the Pyrenees. The Spanish artist, Goya, painted and sketched the obscene cruelties of that war. If Napoleon had avoided Spain – and Russia – who could predict how long he would have been emperor of France and the conquered territories?

In March 1815 he slipped away from Elba and returned to France. That June, in Brussels, the party-loving Duchess of Richmond was giving a ball in honour of the commander in chief, now the Duke of Wellington. A messenger arrived with word that Napoleon was leading his army across the Belgian border.

Wellington, taken by surprise, uttered his famous exclamation, "By God I've been humbugged!"

The ball ended abruptly as the officers scurried off to their units. Would Francis Simcoe, had he lived, been among the Duchess of Richmond's guests, as in Dublin? Would he have been one of the captains who galloped off to Quatre Bras in such haste that he was still in silk hose and dancing pumps?

Instead, like Sir John Moore, his tomb was at a Spanish battlefield, unmarked, in the reddish brown rubble of Badajoz:

> No useless coffin enclosed his breast,
> Not in sheet or in shroud we wound him;
> But he lay like a warrior taking his rest
> With his martial cloak around him.

> Charles Wolfe, from "The Burial of Sir John
> Moore After Corunna".

Notes

Abbreviations
DNB, Dictionary of National Biogoraphy
NA, National Archives, Ottawa
OA, Ontario Archives, Toronto

Frontispiece: OA MS 517, Ser. A-4-1. Lord Moira to EPS, 4 Nov. 1807

Part One: The Canada Years
Chapter 1: Of a Family, Letters and Journals

1. Mary Beacock Fryer, *Elizabeth Posthuma Simcoe: a Biography* Dundurn, Toronto, 1989, Appendix: genealogy by Hilary Arnold, pp. 225-266)

2. Simcoe Papers, Devon Record Office, Exeter, microfilm copies in NA, Reels A605,606,607.

3. OA, Simcoe Papers, reel 1812, F 47-12

4. Mary Quayle Innis ed. *Mrs. Simcoe's Diary*. Toronto, 1965; John Ross Robertson, *The Diary of Mrs. John Graves Simcoe*. Toronto, 1911 and reprint 1973.

Chapter 2: The Simcoes of Wolford Lodge

1. *The Army List*, 1783.

2. Fryer, EPS, Arnold Genealogy pp. 258-59.

3. NA, Reel A605, F.28, E. Gwillim to EPS, 22 March 1798.

4. Innis, p. 43.

5. NA, Reel A606, F29, 19 May 1793.

6. OA, Simcoe Coll., Reel 7-531, Simcoe-Burges, B 1-2, 12 June 1795, MAB to EPS.

Chapter 3: Quebec November 1791, Niagara 1792

1. Innis, p. 29.

2. Ibid., pp. 48, 49.

3. Mary Beacock Fryer, *Allan Maclean: Jacobite General*. Dundurn, Toronto, 1987, pp. 133-37.

4. Innis, p. 54.

5. Ibid., p. 57.

6. NA, reel A606, F29, 23 May 1792, MAB to EPS.

7. Ibid., 27 July.

8. Ibid., 30 June.

9. Robertson, p. 92.

10. Innis, p. 74.

11. Brigadier E.A. Cruikshank. *Simcoe Correspondence*. 5 vols., Toronto, 1923-31, vol. 1, p. 205.

Chapter 4: Newark 1792-1793

1. NA, reel A606, F24, JGS to Charlotte, 22 Aug. 1792.

2. Ibid., Upper Canada, n.d.

3. Innis, p. 82.

4. Ibid., p. 113, 2 Dec. 1793.

5. Ibid., p. 83

6. NA, reel A606, F24, several poems together.

7. Innis, p. 87.

8. NA reel A606, F24, 20 Apr. 1793.

9. Innis, p. 89.

10. NA reel A606, F29, 15 June 1793.

11. Ibid., 20 Nov. 1793.

12. Innis, p. 93.

13. Ibid., p. 97.

14. Ibid., pp. 98, 100.

15. OA, reel 7-531, Simcoe-Burgess B 1-2, Letters from MAB's packets to EPS missing from NA reels, letters missing from the Simcoe Papers, Devon Record office, Exeter, letters of 23 Sept. and 3 Oct. 1793.

16. Innis, pp. 89-90.

Chapter 5: War Clouds

1. Innis, p. 92.

2. Ibid., pp. 104-05.

3. OA, reel 7-531, S-B 1-2, 16 Feb. 1794, MAB's reply to EPS' of 26 Sept. 1793.

4. Innis, p. 110.

5. OA reel, 7-531, B-S 1-2, 29 Dec. 1793.

6. Ibid., 1 Jan., p. 571. Page numbers not always legible.

7. Innis, p. 117.

8. OA, reel 7-531, B-S 1-3, 14 Apr. 1794, p. 621.

9. Innis, pp. 125-26.

10. NA reel A606, F30, n.d., Mrs. Gwillim to Eliza.

11. Innis, p. 127.

12. Ibid., p. 133.

13. Ibid., p. 139.

Chapter 6: Quebec and Return to York

1. Innis, pp. 142, 143.

2. NA, reel A606, F24, JGS to Charlotte, 8 Nov. 1794.

3. Innis, pp. 145, 146.

4. OA, reel 7-531. S-B 1-2, F29, 8 Apr. 1795.

5. Ibid., 18 Apr. 1795.

6. Ibid., 23 Apr. 1795.

7. Innis, p. 148.

8. Ibid, p. 151.

9. Ibid., pp. 152, 153.

10. Ibid., p. 155.

11. OA, reel 7-531, S-B 1-2, F29, 11 Mar. 1795.

12. Ibid., 8 June 1795.

13. Ibid., 12 June 1795.

14. NA reel A606, F29, 31 Jan. 1796.

15. Innis, pp. 158, 159.

16. NA reel A606, F29, 10 Nov. 1796.

17. Innis, p. 160.

18. Ibid., 164, 165.

19. Ibid., p. 167.

20. NA reel A606, F24, n.d., no opening, part is a copy but part is by someone else handing on news.

21. Ibid.

Chapter 7: Last Year in the Canadas

1. Innis, p. 169.

2. OA, letters re EPS, Robertson-Mackenzie Coll. MU-7496, 6 Jan. 1796.

3. NA reel A606, F29, 7 Jan. 1796.

4. Innis,p. 170.

5. Ibid., p. 172.

6. NA reel A606, F29, letters of 2 March, 6 and 27 May 1796.

7. Innis, p. 174.

8. Ibid., p. 176.

9. Ibid., p. 188.

10. Ibid., p. 191.

11. Ibid., pp. 193-94.

12. Ibid., p. 198.

13. Ibid., pp. 205, 206.

Part Two: School Days 1796-1807

Chapter 8: Mr. Copplestone's Pupil and King's School

1. NA reel A607, F30, M. Graves to Eliza, 4 June 1800.

2. Ibid., reel A606, F28, E. Gwillim to EPS 19 Nov. 1796.

3. Fryer, EPS, Arnold genealogy, p. 263.

4. Devon Record Office, #337B/30/1, will of Eliza Simcoe.

5. NA reel A606, F28, E. Gwillim to EPS, 22 March 1798.

6. Ibid., F30, M. Graves to Eliza, ? July 1798.

7. OA, Simcoe Papers, reel 1811, E. Gwillim to EPS, 13 Oct. 1798.

8. Ibid., JGS to FGS, 30 Apr. 1800.

9. NA, reel A607, F30, M. Graves to Eliza, 4 June 1800.

10. Ibid., F7, Caroline to Mrs. Hunt, 9 Jan. 1800. Date should be 1801. Henry was not born until 28 Feb. 1800.

11. The letter is held by the David M. Stewart Museum, Montreal.

12. NA, reel A607, Eliza to Miss Hunt, 23 Jan. 1802.

13. The information on Francis being at King's School was sent by Chris Dracott, of Hemyock, Devon, who obtained it from the school

Chapter 9: Eton College 1804-1807

1. Connor, Tim, "Eton College Preserved", Heritage magazine, Oct/Nov. 1990.

2. OA, F47-12, reel 1812, FGS to EPS, Eton, 28 June 1806.

3. Ibid., FGS to EPS, London, undated. Written before he left London for Ireland.4. Lyte, C.M., *A History of Eton College 1440-1875*. London 1875, pp. 333-336, "The Rebellion of 1768".

5. NA, reel A605, F23, poem by William Boscawen, Esq. to "Colonel" Simcoe on his return from San Domingo.

6. OA, F47-12, reel 1812, FGS to My Dear Mother, Eton, 28 June 1806.

7. Ibid.

8. Ibid., JGS to Eliza, Coimbra, 13 Sept. 1806.

9. Robertson, p. 412. John Bailey, a servant, held this opinion.

10. Exeter Flying Post, 6 Nov. 1806.

11. NA reel A607, F30, M. Graves to Eliza, 20 Nov. 1806, between letters of Oct. 1804 and Dec. 1803,

Part Three: Ensign Francis Simcoe

Chapter 10: Dublin Spring 1808

1. OA F47-12, Moira to EPS, 20 June 1808; War Office 16 July 1808.

2. Riddell, The Hon. William, *The Life of John Graves Simcoe*. Toronto 1926, p. 33.

3. OA F47-12, reel 1812, FGS to My dear Mother, Tues. 15th [Feb. 1808].

4. Ibid.

5. Ibid., J.P. Bastard to EPS, 6 Oct. 1807.

6. Ibid., FGS to My dear mother, no date or place.

7. Ibid., FGS to My dear Mother, 22 Feb. 1808.

8. Ibid., FGS to My dear Mother, Oundle, Fri. Mar. 17.

9. OA F47-12, reel 1812, journal 17 Mar. - 22 Aug. 1808.

10. Ibid.

11. *The Army List* 1808, Irish Officers on Half-Pay; DNB on Atkinson.

12. OA MS 517, series A-4-1, reel 14, Moira to EPS, 25 Mar. 1808.

13. Ibid., FGS to My dear Mother, Sun., 25 Mar. 1808.

14. Ibid., FGS to My dear Mother, Dublin, Mon 5 Apr. 1808.

Chapter 11: At Enniskillen with the Inniskillings

1. OA, Simcoe Papers, F 47-12, reel 1812, journal, May 1808, out of order.

2. Information from the records of the Royal Inniskilling Fusiliers Regmental Museum, The Castle, Enniskillen, courtesy of Margaret Mulligan.

3. Riddell, p. 32.

4. OA F47-12, reel 1812, FGS to M ydear Mother, Enniskillen, 11 Apr. 1808.

5. Fosten, Bryan, *Wellington's Infantry 1*. Osprey Men-at-Arms Series, p. 16, "Pay".

6. OA F47-12, FGS to My ddear Mother, 11 Apr. 1808.

7. Ibid., My dear Mother, Enniskilen, Thur. 12 Apr. 1808.

8. Ibid., FGS to My dear Mother, 12 Apr. 1808, 2nd letter.

9. Fosten, pp. 14-15.

10. OA, F47-12, reel 1812, no opening, cover dated 14 Apr. n. yr.

11. Ibid., FEG to My dear Mother, Sun. 24 Apr. n. yr.

12. Ibid., Littlehales to EPS, Phoenix Park, 4 May 1808.

13. Ibid., FGS to My dear Mother, Enniskillen, 6 May 1808.

14. Ibid., FGS t My dear Mother, 24 and 27 May 1808.

Chapter 12: The March from Enniskillen to the Cove of Cork

1. OA, F47-12, reel 1812, journal May 1808, out of order.

2. Ibid., FGS to My dear Mother, Kells, Thur. 2 June [1808]

3. Ibid., FGS to My dear Mother, Curragh Camp, 8 June 1808.

4. Ibid., FGS to My dear Mother, 6 July 1808.

5. OA, F47-12, reel 1812, Irish Journal starts "After a month in London ..."

6. Ibid., FGS to Dear Sisters, Middleton, 29 Aug. 1808.

7. Ibid., part of FGS' journal to Eliza.

8. Ibid., n.d., part of FGS' journal to Eliza.

9. Ibid., FGS to My dear Mother, Falmouth, 9 Oct. 1808.

10. Ibid., FGS to My dear Mother, Thur. 13 Oct., 1808.

Part Four: Lieutenant Francis Simcoe

Chapter 13: Corunna, Lisbon, Cadiz

1. OA, Simcoe Papers, F47-12, reel 1812. Part of FGS' journal to Eliza, n.d.

2. Ibid., pp. 2, 3, and 4, FGS' journal to Eliza.

3. Ibid., F 47-12, reel 1812, FGS to Dear Mother, Cadiz, 9 Feb. 1809.

4. Ibid.

5. Ibid., FGS to Dear Mother, Cadiz, 24 feb. 1809.

6. Ibid.

7. Ibid., part of Francis' journal, Camarate, 6 Jan., 1809.

8. Ibid., FGS to My dear Mother, Camarate, 23 Mar. 1809.

9. Ibid., p. 5 of Francis' journal, Camarate, 4 Apr. 1809.

10. Ibid.

11. Ibid., FGS to Dearest Sisters, Camarate, 4 Apr. 1809.12. Ibid., FGS to My beloved Mother, Abrantes, 6 May 1809.

Chapter 14: First March to Badajoz

1. OA, F47-12, reel 1812, FGS to My beloved Mother, Abrantes, 6 May 1809.

2. Ibid., FGS to My dear Mother, Carticada[?], 22 May 1809.

3. Ibid., FGS to Dear Mother, Lisbon, Sun. 4 July 1809.

4. Ibid., part of Francis' journal, Badjoz, 8 Oct., 1809.

5. Ibid., FGS to My very dear Mother, p. 4 of a journal, and from a letter dated 25 Aug. 1809.

6. Ibid., 10th page of a journal, with the date 28 Sept., the day the 27th left Lisbon for Badajoz.

7. Ibid., p. 6 of Francis' journal, n.d.

8. Ibid., p. 7 of Francis' jounral.

9. Ibid., p. 8 of Francis' journal.

10. Ibid., pp. 8-9 of Francis' journal.

11. Ibid., page of Francis' journal dated 8 Oct. 1809.

12. Elizabeth Longford, *Wellington: The Years of the Sword*. New York 1969, p. 201.

13. OA, F47-12,ree; 1812, FGS to Beloved Mother, Badajoz, 19 Nov. 1809.

14. Ibid., 19 Nov. 1809.

15. Ibid., FGS to Beloved Mother, Sun. 11 Dec. 1809.

Chapter 15: 1810 First Battle: Bussaco

1. OA F47-12, reel 1812, Beloved Mother, Sun. 11 Dec. 1809.

2. Ibid., Francis' journal, 6 Jan. 1810.

3. Ibid., part of Francis' journal, 15 Jan. 1810.

4. In July he was again off duty, owing to "a second fever", FGS to Dear Mother, Lisbon 20 July 1810.

5. Ibid.

6. Sources for the Battle of Bussaco are from Longford, *Wellington,* pp. 224-232; DNB on Lowry Cole, Rowland Hill; Philip Haythornthwaite and Michael Chapell, *Uniforms of the Peninsular Army, 1807-1814,* Blandford Colour Series, Poole, Dorset, pp. 164-165, Orders of Battle; John William Cole. *Memoirs of British Generals Distinguished During the Peninsular War.* London, 1856, pp. 276-277.

Chapter 16: The Lines of Torres Vedras, Olivenza, Badajoz

1. Longford, Wellington, pp. 235-239.

2. OA F47-12, reel 1812, FGS to My dear Mother, 19 Oct. 1810.

3. Ibid., FGS to Beloved Mother, Azambuja, 26 Nov. 1810.

4. Ibid., FGS to Dear Mother, ?, 22 Dec. 1810.

5. Longford, *Wellington*, p. 238.

6. OA F47-12-0-3, reel 1812, Dear Mother, Castello Branco 4 Mar.

7. Cole, *Memoirs of British Generals*, p. 278.

8. Ibid., p. 278-280.

9. OA F47-12, reel 1812, FGS to My dearest Mother, Montijo, 30 Apr. 1811.

Chapter 17: Acting Captain Francis Simcoe

1. OA F47-12, reel 1812, FGS to Beloved Mother, Badajoz, 12 May 1811.

2. Ibid.

3. Cole, *Memoirs of British Generals*, p. 280.

4. Ibid., pp. 281-287.

5. OA F47-12-0-3, FGS to Beloved Mother, camp at Toro de Moro, 21 June 1811.

6. Ibid.

7. Ibid., FGS to Dear Mother, Aldea del Obispo, 12 Aug. 1811.

8. Ibid.

9. Ibid., FGS to Beloved Mother, Castellejo, 3 Sept. 1811.

10. Ibid., FGS to Beloved Mother, Castellejo de Martin Viejo, 6 Sept. 1811.

11. Ibid., FGS to Charlotte, Albingana[?], 19 Sept. 1811.

12. Ibid., FGS to Harriett [sic] Nave de Haver, 4 Oct. 1811.

Chapter 18: Coimbra 1811 and Ciudad Rodrigo 1812.

1. OA F47-12, ewwl 1812, FGS to Harriett [sic], Nave de Haver, 4 Oct., 1811.

2. Ibid., FGS to Dear Mother, Celorico, 6 Nov. 1811.

3. Ibid., FGS to Dear Mother, Coimbra, 26 Dec. 1811.

4. Ibid.

5. Charles W.C. Oman, *A History of the Peninsular War.* Oxford 1914, vol. 5, pp. 217-225.

6. OA F47-12, reel 1812, no opening or date, 2nd page signed George Mackenzie.

7. DNB. biog. of John Gurwood.

8. Antony Brett-James ed, *Wellington at War 1794-1815.* London 1961, p. 172.

9. OA F47-12, reel 1812, FGS to Dear Mother, Villa de Agua, 1 Feb. 1812.

Chapter 19: The Costly Third Siege, 6 April 1812

1. Oman, *History* vol. 5, p. 218, fn. 1.

2. Ibid.

3. Ibid., p. 224.

4. Ibid., p. 235.

5. OA F47-12, reel 1812, FGS to Beloved Mother, 21 Mar. 1812.

6. Ibid., camp before Badajoz 26 Mar. 1812, no opening.

7. Ibid., Dear Sir, London, 31 Mar. 1812 to C. Flood Esq.

8. Oman, *History,* p. 242.

9. Ibid., p. 244.

Chapter 20: A Warrior Taking His Rest

1. OA F47-12, reel 1812, no opening, signed George Jenkins to EPS, 9 Apr. 1812.

2. Oman, Appendices, p. 594-595.

3. Ibid., pp. 251-252

4. OA, F47-12, reel 1812, Moira to EPS, 27 Apr. 1812.

Bibliography

Primary Sources

Unprinted

Francis Simcoe's journals and letters: Ontario Archives, Simcoe Papers, F47-12, reel 1812, and 5, campaign maps, Spain 1812. These are the most important and extensive primary sources for the work, comparable with Elizabeth Simcoe's diary.

Simcoe-Burges Papers, Ontario Archives, B-1-2, reel 7-531.

Devon Record Office, Simcoe Papers, on microfilm in the National Archives, Ottawa, reels A605, 606 and 607.

Printed

Brett-James, Antony ed. *Wellington at War 1794-1815*. London 1961; Cruikshank, Brigadier E.A. ed. *Simcoe Correspondence*. 5 vols. Toronto, 1923-1931.

Exeter Flying Post. 6 Nov. 1806.

Innis, Mary Quayle. *Mrs. Simcoe's Diary*. Toronto 1965.

Robertson, John Ross. *The Diary of Mrs. John Graves Simcoe*. First published in Toronto, 1911, by William Briggs. Coles' facsimile edition, 1973.

Royal Inniskilling Fusiliers Regimental Museum, The Castle, Enniskillen. Information from the history of the regiment, formerly the 27th Foot.

Secondary Materials

Cole, John William. *Memoirs of British Generals Distinguished During the Peninsular War*. London 1856. Connor, Tim. "Eton College Preserved." Heritage magazine Oct./Nov. 1990.

Cornwell, Bernard. *Sharpe's Company: Richard Sharpe and the Siege of Badajoz, January to April 1812*. London 1983. The Cornwell novels about the indestructible Sharpe give a dramatic picture of the Peninsular War. The map of Badajoz in the 1994 edition is one of the clearest of the battle site *Dictionary of National Biography*. Sir Leslie Stephen and Sir Sidney Lee, eds. London, 1917.

Fosten, Bryan. *Wellington's Infantry 1, and Wellington's Infantry 2*. Osprey Men-at Arms Serces, nos. 114 and 119. London, 1981 and 1982. Fryer, Mary Beacock. *Allan Maclean: Jacobite General*. Toronto, Dundurn, 1987.

Fryer, Mary Beacock. *Allan Maclean: Jacobite General*. Toronto, Dundurn, 1987.

Elizabeth Posthuma Simcoe, a Biography. Toronto, Dundurn, 1989.

Haythornthwaite, Philip, and Chapell, Michael. *Uniforms of the Peninsular War, 1807-1814.* Blandford Colour Series, Poole, Dorset 1978.Longford, Elizabeth. *Wellington: the Years of the Sword.* New York 1969.Lyte, C. M. *A History of Eton College 1440-1875.* London 1875.

Napier, W.F.P. *History of the War in the Peninsula and in the South of France.* 6 vols. London, Cavendish edition, 1886.

Oman, Charles W.C. *A History of the Peninsular War.* Oxford, 1902-1930. 7 vols.

Neillands, Robin. *Napoleon and Wellington: Clash of Arms 1807- 1815.* London 1994.

Riddell, The Hon. William. *The Life of John Graves Simcoe.* Toronto 1926.

The Army List. Various years.

Index